UPDATED & EXPANDED

WALL STREET WORDS

From Annuities to Zero Coupon Bonds

RICHARD J. MATURI

PROBUS
PUBLISHING

Chicago, Illinois
Cambridge, England

This publication is designed to provide accurate and authoritative information in regard to the subject matter covered. It is sold with the understanding that the author and the publisher are not engaged in rendering legal, accounting, or other professional service.

Authorization to photocopy items for internal or personal use, or the internal or personal use of specific clients, is granted by PROBUS PUBLISHING COMPANY, provided that the U.S. $7.00 per page fee is paid directly to Copyright Clearance Center, 222 Rosewood Drive, Danvers, MA 01923, USA; Phone: 1-508-750-8400. For those organizations that have been granted a photocopy license by CCC, a separate system of payment has been arranged. The fee code for users of the Transactional Reporting Service is 1-55738-865-2/95/$00.00 + $7.00.

ISBN 1-55738-865-2

Printed in the United States of America

BB

1 2 3 4 5 6 7 8 9 0

TAQ/BJS

I dedicate this book to two individuals who instilled in me at an early age an appreciation for the stock market. My father, Mario, had me charting stock prices and tracking news of his stocks from the age of seven. My Uncle Rudy, who retired in his thirties and played the stock market for over fifty years, often took me along to watch the action at commodity and stock exchanges from Minneapolis to Chicago, and numerous smoke-filled brokerage houses in between.

Contents

Preface

There are a number of notable finance and investment glossaries, handbooks, and manuals that provide the investor with investment definitions. *Wall Street Words, Rev. Ed.* probes beyond pure definitions and provides concrete examples and strategies that the average investor can use over and over again.

As a companion, this book clarifies the jargon that typically clouds understanding of the intricacies of the financial world. *Wall Street Words, Rev. Ed.* guides you through the complexities of puts and calls, margin, turnaround analysis, annuities, convertible securities, and much more.

Listings appear alphabetically, with numerous cross-references to aid the reader in locating related terms and strategies. Section I contains the listing of terms and easy-to-understand definitions while Section II explores more in-depth discussion, examples, illustrations, and strategies.

Narrative examples help the investor understand how a particular investment strategy works and how to determine whether or not the investment is an appropriate vehicle. Discussions examine the potential rewards as well as the risks associated with various investment paths.

Wall Street Words, Rev. Ed. is required reading for the "hands-on" investor willing to make his or her own investment decisions.

Richard J. Maturi

SECTION I

A

ADR The abbreviation for American Depositary Receipt. A negotiable receipt for shares of a foreign corporation held in the vault of a United States bank. It entitles the owner to all dividends and capital gains. ADR's enable a U.S. citizen to purchase shares of a foreign corporation without trading in overseas markets. For example: A U.S. investor can invest in Benguet Corporation, a Philippine gold mining and engineering company, by purchasing its ADR's which are traded on the New York Stock Exchange. See *ADR* in Section II.

ACCOUNTANT'S OR AUDITOR'S OPINION Report by the independent accountants to the Board of Directors and shareholders describing the scope of the examination of the organization's books. It generally states that the audit examination was made in accordance with generally accepted accounting standards...and such other auditing procedures considered necessary in the circumstances.

In the case of a clean audit, the report will further state, "In our opinion, the aforementioned consolidated financial statements present fairly the consolidated financial position of XXX, Inc. and its subsidiaries at December 31, 1993 and 1994..., in conformity with generally accepted accounting principles applied on a consistent basis."

Depending on the audit findings, the opinion can be unqualified or qualified to specific items. Any qualified opinion bears further investigation. The words "subject to" generally mean trouble. Remember that the company's annual report may signal that the company may be on the verge of very serious financial or operating difficulties.

ACCRUED INTEREST The portion of interest accumulated since the last interest payment. If an investor purchases a bond between interest payment dates, the settlement amount will include the purchase (market) price of the bond plus the amount of interest accrued or accumulated since the last interest payment.

Accrued interest is usually calculated as follows: coupon rate of interest times the number of days since the last payment date.

ACCUMULATED DIVIDEND The amount of dividends due but not paid. Accumulated dividends on cumulative preferred stock must be paid in full before common stock dividends can be paid. See *Cumulative Preferred Stock* in Section I.

ACCUMULATION AREA The price range technicians believe is optimum for purchases of a particular stock. Generally, a stock will not fall below a particular price, providing buying opportunities. A stock's accumulation area may change over time. See also *Distribution Area* in Section I and *Accumulation Area* in Section II for an example of an accumulation area.

ACID-TEST RATIO The acid-test ratio or quick ratio is used to measure corporate liquidity. It is regarded as an improvement over the current ratio which includes inventory, usually not very liquid.

The acid-test formula is stated as current assets less inventory divided by current liabilities. An alternative divides cash, marketable securities, and accounts receivable by current liabilities. Normally an acid-test ratio of 1 to 1 is satisfactory. However, an interruption or slow-down of cash receipts could spell trouble. Conversely, a company with a high acid-test ratio may not be using its capital effectively. Refer to Section II, *Acid-test Ratio* for an example of how to calculate.

ACTIVE MARKET Reference to the market for a particular stock or the overall market characterized by frequent transactions, narrow bid-offer spreads, and relatively high volume. Active markets can absorb large trades more efficiently. Having a feel for the market can help the investor take advantage of the market's efficiencies. A market order in the active market will most likely be executed at a price near the latest quote. However, in a quiet market, an investor might be in for a rude awakening when placing a market buy order and the price jumps substantially due to a lack of sellers.

ADVANCE-DECLINE LINE The ratio of advancing stocks and declining stocks charted by investors to determine the overall trend of the market. A ratio greater than 1 is bullish and less than 1 is bearish. The steepness of the advance-decline indicates the degree of bullish/bearish sentiment.

AFTERTAX BASIS The comparison of yields on tax-free government bonds and taxable corporate bonds. For example, for a person in the 28% tax bracket, he or she would have to earn 10 percent on a taxable corporate bond investment to match the return on a 7.2% tax-free government bond.

AGAINST THE BOX The box in a short sale is the safe deposit box or account of the short seller. In effect, the investor actually owns the security but makes delivery of the short sale by borrowing stock rather than delivering the owned securities.

Reasons for selling short against the box include: tax strategy to get the benefit of long term capital gains (no longer applicable under recent tax law changes), a desire not to disclose ownership, and inability to deliver the owned shares in the required transaction period. See *Short Sale* in Section II.

ALL OR NONE An order by an investor to buy or sell a specified number of units of a security. This prevents the execution of a transaction for only a portion of the securities and eliminates the possibility of paying several commission charges to obtain or sell the specified number of securities.

In underwriting, an all or none agreement gives the issuer the opportunity to cancel the entire issue if the underwriting is not fully subscribed.

AMERICAN DEPOSITARY RECEIPT See *ADR*

ANALYST A person who studies companies and industries in order to make investment buy and sell recommendations. Most analysts work for brokerage firms, bank trust departments, and mutual funds.

ANNUAL BASIS The analytical technique of extrapolating annual performance from data covering periods of less than one year.

ANNUAL REPORT The yearly report issued to stockholders. The SEC requires the company to present an accurate portrayal of events that materially affected operations during the past fiscal year. The report includes a balance sheet, income statement, a description of company operations, and management's discussion of the company and its results.

The annual report provides a wealth of information. Look for discussion of products, pricing, inventory write-downs, acquisitions, divestitures, long-term debt, and working capital. A more detailed report with the SEC and available from the corporate secretary is the 10k for the full year and 10q for quarterly reporting.

ANNUITY An investment contract sold by life insurance companies based on a guarantee of fixed or variable payments for a specified period of time beginning in the future, usually tied to retirement. A fixed annuity will pay out an amount in regular installments. A variable annuity payout will vary with the value of the account. The tax-deferred status of the capital and investment proceeds is a prime investment factor. Recent changes in the tax law make annuities an attractive investment alternative. See Section II, Annuity for a more detailed discussion.

ARBITRAGE The act of benefiting from differences in price of the same commodity, currency, or security traded on two or more markets. The arbitrageur makes money by taking advantage of the price disparity by selling in one market while simultaneously buying in another market. Since the disparity is usually very small, a large volume is required to lock in a significant profit for the arbitrageur.

ASCENDING TOPS A security's chart pattern exhibiting a series of peaks, each higher than the previous peak. Considered bullish, indicating a continuation of rising prices. See *Descending Tops* in Section I. See *Tops and Bottoms* in Section II.

ASKED PRICE The lowest price a dealer or seller is willing to accept. Also called the offering price. Bid is the highest price a dealer or buyer is willing to offer. The difference between bid and asked is called the price spread.

ASSET ALLOCATION Investment technique based on diversifying the portfolio among different types of assets such as stocks, bonds, cash equivalents, precious metals, real estate, and collectibles. See *Diversification* in Section I.

ASSET MANAGEMENT ACCOUNT A one stop account with a bank, brokerage house or savings institution that offers a combination of services such as check writing, money market funds, credit cards, margin loans and other security transactions. All activity is summarized on one monthly statement.

ASSET PLAY A stock investment that value investors find attractive because the value of the firm's assets are not properly reflected in its stock price.

AT THE CLOSE A customer market order to be executed within the last 30 seconds of trading on the exchange. There is no guarantee the order will be executed.

AT THE MARKET An instruction to buy or sell a security as soon as possible at the best available price.

AT THE MONEY An option whose exercise or strike price is the same as the current market price of the underlying security. See also *Exercise Price* and *Strike Price* in Section I.

AT THE OPENING An instruction to a broker to buy or sell a security at the price that applies when the exchange opens. If the order cannot be executed at that time, it is automatically canceled.

AUTHORIZED SHARES The maximum number of shares a company can legally create under its articles of incorporation. The number of authorized shares can be increased by action of the firm's Board of Directors.

AVERAGE DOWN, AVERAGE UP Strategies used to purchase stocks over a period of time. To average down, an investor will make an initial purchase at a set price but will wait for downside movement before adding to the stock position. To average up, an investor will purchase equal quantities of the same security as the price rises thus lowering the overall average cost below the current market price.

AWAY FROM THE MARKET An order that cannot be currently executed because it contains a limit bid, or a limited offer, above prevailing quotes for the security. This strategy is profitable in thinly traded securities where a market order can trigger your sale or purchase.

B

BACK-END LOAD A charge paid at redemption of a mutual fund or annuity. Usually designed to discourage the withdrawal of funds from an investment. See *Front-end Load* in Section I.

BALANCED MUTUAL FUND A mutual fund that attempts to earn an acceptable return consistent with the low-risk strategy of investing in a mixed portfolio of common stocks, preferred stocks, and bonds. Usually a balanced fund outperforms a pure equity fund when stocks are falling and lags pure equity funds in a rising market.

BANKRUPTCY The insolvency of an individual or organization. A Chapter 7 bankruptcy allows the court to appoint a trustee empowered to make management changes, secure financing, and otherwise operate the business. A Chapter 11 bankruptcy allows the debtor organization protection from creditors while attempting to reorganize the business. Restructuring of debt, labor renegotiation, and new business relationships and terms with suppliers and customers normally occur during this restructuring.

BASIS The original cost of an investment including all acquisition costs such as commissions. In commodities, the difference between the price of the item being hedged and the price of the futures contract.

BASIS POINT The measure used to determine movement in bond yield. A basis point equals 0.01% yield. A bond whose yield has increased from 9.25% to 11.05% had an increase of 180 basis points.

BASIS PRICE The cost of an investment used to determine capital gains or losses.

BEAR An investor who believes that stock prices will decline either for the market in general or for a particular security. An active bear will sell stocks short, purchase puts, or sell an uncovered call to capitalize on the anticipated decline. See *Bull* in Section I.

BEAR MARKET A stretch of time from several months to several years during which stock prices tumble.

BEARER SECURITY A security payable to the person possessing it. Coupon bonds were bearer bonds in that the clipped coupons could be redeemed by anyone. Most securities are now registered in the name of the owner and can be transferred only upon proper endorsement.

BELLWETHER A security that takes a leadership position in the direction of the stock market in general or for a particular industry. The phrase, "As General Motors goes, so goes the nation," was predicated on its bellwether position in regard to the national economy.

BETA A measure of the price volatility of a specific stock in relation to the market in general. The S&P 500 Composite Stock Index has a beta of 1. A more volatile stock would have a beta greater than 1 and would rise and decline faster than the S&P 500. Generally, stocks with betas greater than 1 are more risky while stocks with betas less than 1 have more conservative followings.

BID PRICE The highest price at which a dealer or buyer is willing to pay for a security. The *Asked Price* is the lowest price at which a dealer or seller is willing to accept. The difference between bid and asked is called the price spread.

BLIND POOL A limited partnership that does not disclose the investments the general partner intends to pursue. In contrast, a specified real estate pool, lists the properties acquired, prices paid, and rental income. Blind pools may be used to acquire real estate, high-tech companies, and to fund research and development.

BLOCK TRADING The purchase or sale of large quantities of stock. Typically, trades involving 10,000 or more shares and $200,000 in value are considered block trades.

BLUE CHIP Stocks of the highest quality with a long record of earnings and dividend growth. Usually well-known industry leaders known for quality management.

BOND A long-term debt security obligating the issuer to pay interest and repay the principal. Both corporations and governments issue bonds. The holder holds rights to receive interest and return of principal but has no ownership rights in the issuing corporation.

A convertible bond is exchangeable for corporate stock at a predetermined conversion factor. Therefore, a convertible bond will more closely follow the price actions of the company's common stock. See *Convertible Bond* in Section II.

A secured bond is backed by collateral (corporate assets) while an unsecured bond is backed by the faith and credit of the issuer.

In the event of bankruptcy, bondholders have precedent over stockholders. Some bond issues may be subordinate to others so make sure you know the status of your bond holdings in the case of a bankruptcy.

BOND RATING The credit worthiness of a bond issuer as determined by one of several rating services. Moody's Investors Service, Standard and Poor's Corporation, and Fitch Investor's Service, Inc. evaluate bond issuers' financial strength and cash flow with respect to projected interest payments and principal repayment. Ratings range from AAA or Aaa (highest) to D (in default). Bonds rated below B are not investment grade and are termed "junk bonds" in the trade.

BOND RATIO The measure of a corporation's leverage relating bonds as a percentage of total capitalization. The bond ratio is determined by dividing all bonds due after one year by the total of those bonds plus stockholders' equity. Different industries have different normal bond ratios.

Utilities, for instance, have a high bond ratio. Compare the bond ratio of stocks you hold with other companies in the same industry to determine if the company may be over-leveraged. See *Capitalization Ratio* and *Debt-to-equity Ratio* in Section I.

BOOK VALUE The value of a particular asset or the value of the company as carried on the accounting records of the business. Company book value is determined by the reducing the value of the assets by the intangibles and then deducting all liabilities. Since book value may not approximate real market value, book value per share analysis is a crude method utilized in seeking out undervalued stocks.

BOTTOM The lowest price of a security, commodity, or the market in general for a specified period of time.

Also considered a support level beyond which the price of a security or the market has failed to penetrate after reaching the price range several times. Market technicians chart stock fluctuations seeking bottoms to aid in timing of stock purchases. See *Tops and Bottoms* in Section II for chart examples.

BOTTOM UP INVESTING Investment strategy concentrating on individual stock fundamentals before looking at the big picture implications of different economic scenarios. See *Top-down Investing* in Section I.

BREAK A significant and rapid drop in price of a security or the market in general.

BREAKOUT The action of a security or market rising above a resistance level or dropping below a support level thereby breaking the previous trading pattern. See *Tops and Bottoms* in Section II for chart examples.

BULL An investor who believes that stock prices will rise for the market in general or for a particular security. An active bull will purchase shares outright or purchase calls to capitalize on the anticipated advance. See also *Bear* in Section I.

BULL MARKET A stretch of time, from several months to years, in which stock prices rise.

C

CALLS The provision allowing a bond or preferred stock issuer to recall the issue before maturity (if applicable). The call provision specifies the earliest the issue can be called and spells out other terms and conditions. When purchasing bonds which have appreciated substantially over the maturity value, investigate the call provision in order to avoid having the bond called at less than current market value.

Issuers will recall securities when it is advantageous to retire older issues with higher interest rates than current financing options.

CALL OPTIONS A contract giving the holder the right to buy the underlying security at a specific price during a specified period of time. The exercise price of the option is called the "striking price." See *Call Options* in Section II for further discussion and call investment strategies.

CAPITALIZATION RATIO The breakdown of a company's long-term financing showing what percentage is common stock, preferred stock and bonds. The analysis reflects the amount of leverage used by the company. See *Bond Ratio* and *Debt-to-equity Ratio* in Section I.

CASH EQUIVALENT Fund asset type containing short-term, liquid investments having a maturity of less than one year. Usually used for temporary investment purposes pending an investment or distribution. Money market accounts at brokerages are denominated in cash equivalents.

CASH FLOW The flow of funds in and out of an operating business. Normally calculated as net income plus depreciation and other non-cash items.

Cash flow analysis is an excellent investment tool in determining the company's ability to meet upcoming cash obligations and as an evaluation tool to ferret out undervalued companies. See *Cash Flow Analysis* in Section II.

CASH RATIO The cash ratio is used to measure liquidity. It is calculated as the sum of cash and marketable securities divided by current liabilities. It indicates how a company can meet current creditor claims.

CHARTING A technical analysis technique used in tracking price trends in order to determine patterns in price movements. A person who charts stocks is termed a chartist in the trade. See *Technical Analysis* in Section I.

CIRCUIT BREAKER Market control techniques enacted by stock and commodity exchanges to restore order to the market by temporarily halting trading when the market has dropped by a specific amount during a specific period of time. Pressure for circuit breakers came in the wake of the October 1987 and October 1989 precipitous market drops.

CLOSE The period just prior to the termination of a trading day at which orders can be filled within the closing price range. Also the final trade of a security for the day.

CLOSED-END FUND An investment fund with a limited number of shares outstanding. Closed-end funds are usually traded on listed exchanges or over-the-counter. See *Open-end*

Investment Company in Section I. See *Closed-end Fund* in Section II.

COMMODITY FUTURE A commodity contract that obligates the holder to buy or sell a designated unit measure of a commodity at a predetermined price by a specified settlement date.

COMMON STOCK Class of corporate ownership usually entitled to vote for the board of directors and other issues of importance. The board can vote cash and stock dividends. Preferred stockholders, bond holders, and creditors hold prior claim to corporate assets in the event of a bankruptcy or liquidation

COMMON STOCK EQUIVALENT Securities that may be exchanged for common stock. In some cases, additional cash must also be exchanged. Common stock equivalents include convertible preferred stock, convertible bonds, rights and warrants. Common stock equivalents are used in computing the diluted earnings per share. See *Dilution* in Section I.

COMMON STOCK RATIO The relationship of common stock to the total capitalization of the company. It is calculated by dividing the sum of common stock, paid-in surplus and retained earnings by the total capitalization.

CONTINGENT LIABILITIES Potential obligations that will materialize only if certain events occur in the future. Contingent liabilities can arise from pending lawsuits, disputed claims, cases under appeal, possible tax assessments, discounted notes receivable, and contract disputes. For instance, government contractors can have their contract payments reduced if profits exceed federal government limits.

Contingent liabilities should be disclosed in the financial statements or accompanying footnotes. When evaluating a company for investment, be sure to read the footnotes, they contain a wealth of information.

CONTRARIAN INVESTING The strategy of investing in securities, companies and/or industries that are currently out of favor with the general investing public and institutions. Types of contrary investing include searching out undervalued situations, turnaround candidates and cyclical companies nearing the bottom of the trough. See *Turnaround* in Section II.

CONVERSION PREMIUM The difference between the cost of a convertible and the market price of the underlying stock.

CONVERTIBLE Securities (preferred stocks and bonds) that are exchangeable into common stock at the option of the holder under specified terms and conditions. The conversion ratio specifies the number of shares the holder receives upon surrender of the convertible security. The conversion price is the effective price paid for the common stock when conversion occurs. See *Convertible* in Section II for further discussion and investment strategy.

COUPON BOND A bond issued with detachable coupons for redemption of interest. The coupons are "clipped" and presented for payment by the holder. A coupon bond is a bearer bond, meaning the person in possession of the bond and its coupons is entitled to the interest payments and return of principal. Today most bonds are registered in the name of the holder and transfer must be properly endorsed.

COVER The act of closing out your position. For example, a person who has sold short will purchase the shorted stock to close out or cover the short position.

COVERED CALL A call option written by an investor holding the shares of the underlying stock. A call option written with the writer not owning the underlying shares is a naked option. See *Call Options* in Sections I and II.

CUMULATIVE PREFERRED STOCK A special preferred stock class that accumulates unpaid dividends for future payment. Cumulative preferred stock has prior rights to dividends over common stock; therefore, the omitted cumulative preferred dividends must be paid before common stock dividends can be paid.

Investment in turnaround situations with cumulative preferred dividends in arrears can provide a nice kicker when the company's successful turnaround allows it to resume dividend payments. See *Accumulated Dividends* in Section I.

CURRENCY FUTURES Contracts for future delivery of a specified unit of foreign currency at a fixed price in U.S. dollars at a specified date.

CURRENT RATIO A liquidity ratio calculated by dividing current assets by current liabilities. A refinement of this ratio, to remove the impact of inventory, resulted in the acid-test or quick ratio. See *Acid-Test Ratio* in Section II for an example and comparison of both the current ratio and acid-test ratio.

CURRENT YIELD The effective interest rate based on the annual interest earned divided by the current market price of the bond. For example, a $1,000 bond selling for $850 and paying $80 a year interest has a current yield or 9.41% (80/850). The coupon rate in this example is 8% (80/1,000). See *Yield* in Section I.

CUSTOMER'S LOAN CONSENT Agreement between a brokerage and margin customer allowing the broker to borrow margined securities (up to the debit balance of the customer) for use in delivery against short sales by other customers or in the event of certain failed deliveries.

CYCLICAL Industries and stocks that tend to follow the fortunes of the economy. When the economy prospers, these industries and stocks tend to rebound and vice versa. The automotive and steel industries and stocks are considered cyclical. Shrewd and patient investors pick up these stocks at attractive prices when the economy is experiencing a trough only to unload them later after late-comers bid up their prices.

D

DAILY TRADE LIMIT On commodity and option markets, the maximum amount a contract is allowed to rise or fall in one day.

DATE OF RECORD The effective date that determines which shareholder officially owns the stock and is thus eligible to receive the cash or stock dividend.

DAY ORDER A market order to buy or sell securities that expires if not executed before the end of the trading day in which it is entered.

DEBENTURE A debt instrument backed only by the full faith and credit of the issuing company. Examples include unsecured bonds and commercial paper.

DEBT-TO-EQUITY RATIO The relationship of a company's total debt to total shareholders' equity as a measure of leverage. It can be used to estimate the vulnerability of future earnings to variation. See *Bond Ratio* and *Capitalization Ratio* in Section I.

DEEP DISCOUNT BOND A bond originally issued at a par value of $1,000 and now trading at less than 80% (20% discount) of par value.

DEFENSIVE SECURITIES OR INDUSTRIES Corporate securities and industries that are characterized as being least affected by recessions and general economic downturns. Some defensive industries include food, utility, and other required services or products.

DELAYED OPENING The postponed trading in a stock due to a large imbalance in buy and sell orders, usually due to a takeover or other substantial event.

DEPOSITARY RECEIPT See *ADR* (American Depositary Receipt).

DESCENDING TOPS A security's chart pattern exhibiting a series of peaks, each lower than the previous peak. Considered bearish, indicating a continuation of declining prices. See *Ascending Tops* in Section I. See *Tops and Bottoms* in Section II.

DIFFERENTIAL The excess charge by dealers for processing "odd lot" transactions. An odd lot is less than 100 share multiples for stocks and less than $1,000 or $5,000 multiples for bonds. See *Odd Lot* and *Round Lot* in Section I. The odd lot differential charge is generally 1/8 of a point.

DILUTION The calculation of earnings per share taking into account all convertible securities and common stock equivalents. See also *Common Stock Equivalent* in Section I.

DIP A temporary drop in security prices during a sustained market rally. Astute investors follow individual stock trading and price patterns to take advantage of price dips.

DISCLOSURE Corporate information release required by the Securities and Exchange Commission and the appropriate stock exchange. The information may be either positive or negative or have no material effect. For instance, disclosure of insider sales of company stock may be for personal reasons such as needing money to send a child to college or it may signal lackluster future earnings for the company.

DISCOUNT BROKER A brokerage house that charges substantially lower commissions for executing orders to buy and sell securities. Many discount brokers set up business after "May Day" (May 1, 1975) when the Securities and Exchange Commission ended fixed commissions. Today many banks and other financial institutions also offer discount brokerage services.

DISCRETIONARY ACCOUNT An account authorizing the broker to execute security transactions without providing the client with prior information on the trade to be executed. Unless an investor has complete faith in the broker and the broker's investment judgment, discretionary accounts can lead to disagreements not to mention disappointing investment returns.

DIVERSIFICATION The spreading of investment risk by owning different types of securities, precious metals, and money market funds. Stocks are spread between different companies across several industries. See *Asset Allocation* in Section I.

DIVIDEND A distribution of profits to shareholders. Dividends are usually paid quarterly at a set rate which is reviewed periodically by the Board.

DIVIDEND PAYOUT RATIO The percent of current earnings paid out to stockholders in cash dividends. See *Yield* in Section I.

DIVIDEND REINVESTMENT PLAN Investment offered by many companies allowing shareholders to reinvest their dividends in more shares of the company stock. Usually brokerage fees are absorbed by the company and some plans also discount the stock price. See *Dividend Reinvestment Plan* in Section II.

DOLLAR COST AVERAGING Investment strategy based on purchasing securities over a period of time by investing a fixed-dollar amount at specific intervals. When the price is lower, more shares or units of the security are purchased than when prices are higher. See *Investment Club* in Section II.

DOUBLE BOTTOM A security's chart pattern exhibiting successive lows at the same price level. The market technicians' interpretation is that the stock has substantial support at that level and should not break through to a new low. A breakthrough is a signal for continued price declines. See *Double Top* in Section I. See *Tops and Bottoms* in Section II.

DOUBLE TOP A security's chart pattern exhibiting successive highs at the same price level. The market technicians' interpretation is that the stock has substantial resistance to moving above this level. A breakthrough is a signal for continued price appreciation. See *Double Bottom* in Section I. See *Tops and Bottoms* in Section II.

DOW JONES INDUSTRIAL AVERAGE (DJIA) The most renowned price-weighted market indicator. The DJIA measures the stock-price movements of 30 actively traded U.S. corporations. The average is computed by adding the prices of these 30 stocks and dividing by a divisor adjusted for stock splits, stock dividends and mergers. Although changes to the DJIA company listing have been relatively infrequent, recent changes have been made to allow the DJIA to more accurately reflect the nation's changing economy from heavily industrial to service-related. See *Stock Indexes* in Section II to get a current listing of the DJIA.

DOW THEORY A forecasting system based on interpretation of the action of the Dow-Jones Industrial and Transportation Averages. First formulated by Charles Dow and S.A. Nelson at the turn of the century, the Dow Theory maintains that a major stock market trend must be confirmed by a similar trend in the Dow Jones Industrial Average and the Dow Jones Transportation Average. According to Dow Theory, no primary trend—one that will last more than a year—exists unless both Dow Jones averages reach new highs or lows.

DOWNTICK The sale of a security at a price lower than the previous sale.

E

E/P RATIO Earnings-price ratio is the reciprocal of the price-earnings ratio (P/E Ratio). The E/P ratio is the relationship of earnings per share to the current market price. See *Price/Earnings Ratio* in Section I.

EARNINGS PER SHARE Net after tax income of a corporation applicable to each share of common stock. If there are outstanding convertible securities, the unadjusted earnings per share are called primary earnings. Earnings per share adjusted to account for convertible securities are called fully diluted earnings. See *Dilution* and *Common Stock Equivalent* in Section I.

ECONOMIC INDICATORS Economic statistics reflecting the general direction of the economy. Some indicators are termed leading indicators because they tend to lead or forecast the direction of the economy or business cycle. The stock market is known as a leading indicator.

Other examples of economic indicators include: Utility usage, unemployment rate, balance of trade, interest rates, inventory changes, and building permits.

EFFECTIVE RATE The yield on a debt security based on its purchase price. The effective rate and the coupon rate may vary substantially depending on the price of the debt security, which takes into account current interest rates and changes in the company's financial position since issuance of the debt security.

EFFICIENT MARKET A market which takes into account all known information quickly and accurately. Efficient market advocates consider all information automatically reflected in the price of a security; therefore, it is impossible to "discover" undervalued companies.

EQUITY A security possessing ownership interests in a corporation. Usually called stock. Common stock has no preference in the payment of dividends or rights in the case of bankruptcy. Preferred stock can have preference in dividends, voting rights, and bankruptcy rights over common stock.

EQUIVALENT BOND YIELD The measurement of yield on U.S. Treasury bills on an annualized basis if held to maturity.

Used to compare yields on Treasury bills to yields on other instruments such as debt securities and money market securities.

For example, for a 10%, $10,000 face value U.S. Treasury bill with a 90-day maturity selling for $9,800, the equivalent bond yield would be calculated as follows:

$$\frac{\$200}{9,800} \times \frac{365 \text{ days}}{90 \text{ days}} = 8.3\%$$

EQUIVALENT TAXABLE YIELD Comparison of taxable yield on a corporate bond with the non-taxable yield on a municipal bond taking into account the taxpayer's tax bracket.

EX-DIVIDEND The date on which the purchaser of a stock does not receive the dividend. Any purchase of the stock on that date or after will be ex-dividend. Usually the opening price of the stock will be reduced by the value of the dividend.

EXERCISE To act upon the right the stock option entitles the holder. In the case of a stock call, the holder can exercise the right to purchase the security at a specified price. The holder of a put can exercise the right to sell a security at a specified price. The act of exercising an option will entail paying a commission as if the transaction were a regular purchase or sale of a security.

EXERCISE PRICE Also called striking price. The price at which an option or futures contract can be executed according to the terms of the contract.

EXPIRATION DATE The last day an option can be exercised after which the option expires worthless.

EXTRAORDINARY ITEM Items disclosed in the annual report as nonrecurring items which materially affected financial results. Examples include expenses related to acquisitions or plant shutdowns, results of legal proceedings, or unanticipated tax benefits.

Pay particular attention to extraordinary items when evaluating a company for investment. Extraordinary items can disclose the efforts of past sins (bad management decisions) of the company. Examine several years' annual reports and 10k's to get a feel for a company's extraordinary items. For example, the sale or writedown of a division in the current year may follow anticipated high earnings from the same division in earlier company reports.

F

FACE VALUE The value as stated on the certificate of a bond, note or other financial instrument. This is the amount which the instrument will be redeemed for at maturity. Bonds may be called early at different redemption values as stated in the call provision of the bond indenture. Prior to maturity, bonds may trade above or below face value in reaction to current interest rates and the investing public's perception of the underlying company's financial position and ability to repay the bond issue. Also called par value.

FAIL POSITION Position resulting from the failure of a customer to deliver the sold securities to their broker for delivery to the purchasing customer's broker. A broker will have a net fail position. If other brokers did not deliver enough securities to satisfy his customers' purchases it will be a fail-to-receive position. If he did not deliver enough securities to other brokers, he will have a fail-to-deliver position.

FNMA (FANNIE MAE) The nickname for the Federal National Mortgage Association and its debt securities. Fannie Mae was created to purchase and resell mortgages issued by the Federal Housing Administration (FHA). See *GNMA (Ginnie Mae)* in Section I.

FDIC The Federal Deposit Insurance Corporation (FDIC) created by the U.S. government to insure savings and time deposits in member banks. Established under the Banking Act of 1933, FDIC now covers up to $100,000 per separate account at each insured bank.

FEDERAL RESERVE The federal banking system consisting of twelve independent reserve banks: Atlanta, Boston, Chicago, Cleveland, Dallas, Kansas City, Minneapolis, New York, Philadelphia, Richmond, San Francisco and St. Louis.

The Federal Reserve Board (FRB) serves as the governing body of the Federal Reserve System; its seven members appointed by the President of the United States and confirmed by the U.S. Senate. The Board sets policy on reserve requirements, the discount rate charged to member banks, and attempts to control monetary policy through the loosening or tightening of credit and interest rates.

The Federal Open Market Committee (FOMC) sets short-term monetary policy for the Federal Reserve. It is comprised of six Federal Reserve Banks.

Actions of the Federal Reserve are watched closely by both market fundamentalists and technicians.

FILL The execution of an order to purchase or sell a security.

FILL OR KILL A limit order to purchase or sell a security that instructs the broker to cancel the order if it cannot be executed immediately. Fill or kill orders are generally entered for large trades which may trigger a significant price change if not executed immediately.

FILTER RULE A technical trading rule specifying a breakpoint for an individual stock or market average. Trades are executed when the price change is greater than the filter.

FINANCIAL FUTURE A futures contract on interest-sensitive securities or financial assets. Examples include Treasury bonds, certificates of deposit, stock indexes, and currencies.

FIRST CALL DATE The earliest date at which the issuer can call a debt security for redemption. The bond indenture will spell out all call dates, call prices, and applicable call terms and conditions.

FISCAL YEAR The twelve month accounting period for determining the profit or loss for an entity. The fiscal year may or may not correspond to the regular calendar year. Many companies maintain fiscal years different from calendar years due to the physical nature or business cycle of their industry.

FIXED ANNUITY Investment contract sold by insurance companies which guarantees fixed payments for life or for a specified period. In contrast, a variable annuity's payments vary depending on the underlying portfolio. See *Variable Annuity* in Section I and *Annuity* in Sections I and II.

FIXED-CHARGED COVERAGE Analysis of a corporation's income before interest and taxes to interest on bonds and other long-term debt. Bond rating services use fixed-charge coverage in determining the bond safety and thus its rating.

FIXED-INCOME SECURITY A security with specific payment dates and amounts. Bonds and preferred stocks are fixed-income securities.

FLAG Technical analysis chart pattern designating consolidation before a breakout. The chart of price fluctuations in a narrow trading range resembles a flag and is preceded and followed by steep price advances or declines.

FLASH Delay in market tape more than five minutes due to heavy trading volume. A flash interrupts the tape display to report the current or flash price of a heavily traded security.

FLAT BOND A bond that trades without accrued interest. Bonds that are in default trade flat. Accrued interest will be paid to the buyer if and when the accrued interest is paid, no interest is paid to the seller of a bond trading flat.

FLAT MARKET Price action of a security or the market in general that exhibits a horizontal price movement due to little or no market activity.

FLOAT The number of shares held by the investing public. Stocks with small float are susceptible to sharp price movements.

FLOOR BROKER A registered member of the exchange who executes buy and sell orders on the floor of the exchange for customers of his member firm.

FLOOR TRADER A registered member of an exchange who trades for his or her private account.

FORCED CONVERSION A conversion instigated by the issuer calling in the security for redemption. A forced conversion generally happens when the underlying stock has risen sharply and the convertible has risen above the call price. The owner of the convertible has a choice of converting, selling the security or accepting the call price which is lower than current market price.

FORMULA INVESTING Investment strategy attempting to limit emotional decision making. Most formula investing strategies are based on timing or price levels. For example, dollar cost averaging and apportioning investment between stocks and bonds depending on stock and bond price relationships.

FORWARD CONTRACT A contract for the delivery of a specified commodity, security, currency or financial instrument at a specified rate at a future specified date.

FOURTH MARKET A computerized communications network linking institutional investors for purposes of executing trades between the institutions without using a brokerage firm.

FRACTIONAL DISCRETION ORDER A buy or sell order for securities that gives the broker discretion to execute the order within a specified fraction of a point. For example, a fractional discretion order to purchase 500 shares of XYZ Corporation at $6 a share, discretion one-quarter point, means that the broker can execute the order at any price up to and including $6.25 a share. The customer knows up front what the maximum cost will be and does not run the risk of paying too much if the price surges or of missing the purchase if the stock opens at 6 1/4 and never reaches $6 a share.

FREDDIE MAC The nickname for the Federal Home Loan Mortgage Corporation (FHLMC), which establishes and serves as a secondary market for the conventional mortgage market and thrift institutions.

FREE CREDIT BALANCE Cash in a customer's brokerage account which may be withdrawn by the customer at any time. Funds received in short sales are held in escrow and are not part of the free credit balance.

FRONT-END LOAD A charge paid upon the initial purchase of a mutual fund or annuity. The investor should consider the return needed to recover this front-end charge and still be an attractive investment. See *Back-end Load* In Section I.

FULLY DILUTED EARNINGS PER SHARE The adjusted earnings per share for common stock after taking into account all convertible securities. When the convertible securities have not been converted, earnings will be reported for both primary earnings and fully diluted earnings per share. See *Dilution, Earnings Per Share* and *Primary Earnings* in Section I.

FULL-SERVICE BROKER A brokerage firm providing total investment and financial services to its customers. Full-service brokers generally work on a commission basis. In contrast to discount brokers, full-service broker fees are higher to cover the cost of investment research and financial advice given the client.

FUNDAMENTAL ANALYSIS The analytical approach to investing that is based on the intrinsic value of the company. The underlying economic value of the company is determined by review of the company's balance sheet and income statements. Fundamental analysis attempts to predict a company's future performance based on the analysis of its fundamental strengths and weaknesses. Analysis of a company's financial ratios, for instance, may signal an undervalued situation. See *Technical Analysis* in Section I. Also refer to *Fundamental Analysis* in Section II.

FUTURES CONTRACT An agreement providing for the future exchange of a financial asset or commodity at an agreed-upon price in a future determined month. A futures contract obligates the seller to sell the underlying financial instrument or commodity and the buyer to purchase the underlying financial instrument or commodity at the predetermined price on settlement date. The contract can be sold to another investor to close out the position. Do not confuse options with futures contracts. With an option, the buyer may choose to exercise the option, while a futures buyer is committed to fulfill the futures contract. See *Option* in Section I.

FUTURES EXCHANGE A marketplace for the trading of futures contacts in financial instruments or commodities. Certain futures exchanges specialize in different kinds of futures contracts, for example, The Chicago Rice and Cotton Exchange. Other well-known futures exchanges include The Commodity Exchange (Comex), The Chicago Mercantile Exchange, The International Monetary Market, and The New York Futures Exchange. See *Spot Market* in Section I.

FUTURES OPTION An option contract on a futures contract. For example, an investor could buy a call option on interest rate futures.

G

GNMA (Ginnie Mae) The nickname for the Government National Mortgage Association. The GNMA was established in 1968 when FNMA (Fannie Mae) became a New York Stock Exchange-listed corporation. GNMA manages a program of mortage-backed securities in order to attract funds for secondary mortgages and provide liquidity for existing mortgage securities. See *FNMA (Fannie Mae)* and *Ginnie Mae Pass-through* in Section I.

GAP The pattern of a stock or commodity chart when the price for one day's trading does not overlap the previous day's price range. The gap can be a forerunner of a dramatic price movement for the stock or commodity depending on the nature of the investment news that caused the gap. A downside gap could be triggered by substantially lower earnings results than originally predicted. See *Gap* in Section II for an illustration chart of a gap.

GENERAL OBLIGATION BOND A municipal bond secured by the full faith and credit of the issuing body. It is generally repaid through the taxing power of the municipality.

GILT-EDGED A corporate security noted for its ability to pay uninterrupted dividends or interest. Gilt-edged denotes a superior quality investment security.

GINNIE MAE PASS-THROUGH A Government National Mortgage Association (GNMA) security backed by a pool of mortgages and allows the pass-through of principal and interest payments on the underlying mortgages to the investor bondholders. Homeowners make their mortgage payments to the pass-through investors. GNMA insures that the mortgage payments (both principal and interest) will be made on time.

GLASS-STEAGALL ACT Federal law enacted in 1933 prohibiting commercial banks from owning brokerage firms and engaging in underwriting corporate and municipal revenue bond securities. The banks have circumvented a number of the Glass-Steagall provisions. Introduction of financial institution discount brokerages, commercial paper and money market funds under a holding company umbrella are some examples.

GOLDEN PARACHUTE Provisions passed by the board of directors providing lucrative contracts for key executives. Golden parachutes provide security for executives in the case of an unfriendly takeover. They are now part of poison-pill provisions geared at preventing takeover efforts. The golden parachute provisions may include a bonus, general termination pay package, stock options, and a consulting agreement.

GOOD DELIVERY Delivery of a certificate that has met all the necessary requirements to enable proper transfer of title to the purchasing investor.

GOOD-TILL-CANCELED ORDER A limit or stop order placed by an investor that instructs the broker that the order shall remain in effect until filled or canceled by the investor. Some brokerage houses automatically cancel Good-Till-Canceled orders (GTC) after thirty days. In addition, stocks trading under one dollar are usually restricted to Day Orders. GTC orders are very handy for the investor who wants to purchase or sell a stock at a particular price and does not mind waiting for the stock to reach that price level. A GTC order helps insure the investor the stock trade will be executed at the specified price even though he or she cannot actively follow the stock's price on a timely basis.

GRANTOR The term for the options trader who either sells a call or put option and earns premium income. The grantor sells the right to buy a security at a specific price with a call and the right to sell a security at a specific price with a put. See *Premium Income* in Section I.

GREENMAIL Payment by a takeover target to prevent an unfriendly takeover, usually involving repurchase of stock for substantially more than the acquiring company paid for the investment position.

GROSS SPREAD The difference between public offering price of a new securities issue and the proceeds received by the issuer. The difference is composed of the underwriter's discount, manager's fee and the selling group concession or discount.

GROWTH FUND A mutual fund specializing in growth stocks. Like their growth stock counterparts, growth funds tend to rise more rapidly in bull markets and fall more sharply in bear markets.

GROWTH INVESTMENTS Companies or industries whose earnings are projected to rise substantially above the performance of other companies or industries. A growth stock tends to invest its capital and utilize its assets to realize a rate of return well in excess of its cost of capital.

GUARANTEED BOND A bond which has its principal and interest payments guaranteed by someone other than the bond issuer. The guarantee can limit the duration of interest payments guaranteed. Parent companies often guarantee the bonds issued by a subsidiary. Look at the financial stability for the firm offering the guarantee.

GUARANTEE INCOME CONTRACT Contract issued by insurance companies to pension and profit-sharing plans that guarantees a specific rate of return for the contract life. The retirement plans lock in an acceptable return while the insurance company assumes the investment risks including market movement, interest rate changes, and credit risks for the underlying security portfolio. The insurance company stands to gain if the actual return on investments exceeds the guaranteed rate of return.

H

HEAD AND SHOULDERS A stock or commodity chart pattern outlining the head and shoulders of a person. Technical analysts interpret the pattern as signaling a price trend reversal. As the price patterns forms the right shoulder, technicians view the trend bearish and a forebearer of lower stock prices. In contrast, a reverse head and shoulders stock pattern has the head near the bottom of the chart, indicating a price rise in the future. See *Head and Shoulders* in Section II for an illustration.

HEDGING An investment position utilizing offsetting securities positions to minimize the risk of a financial loss. Examples include a position in a futures market to offset the position held in a cash market, holding a security and selling short against the box, and a call option against a shorted stock. A perfect hedge eliminates the possibility for a future gain or loss. An imperfect hedge insures against a portion of the loss. See *Short Against The Box* in Section I.

HIGH FLYER A highly-speculative and over-priced stock whose price varies sharply over a short period of time. Usually the result of rumors involving reports of technological breakthroughs in high-technology issues, medical breakthroughs in biotechnology stocks or significant mineral deposit finds in mining stocks

HIGH-GRADE BOND A bond receiving AAA (Aaa) or AA (Aa2) ratings from the bond rating services.

HIGH-PREMIUM CONVERTIBLE BOND A long-term convertible bond offering an attractive interest rate which commands a premium substantially over the value at which it is convertible into common stock.

HIGH-TECH STOCK Securities of companies in high technology industries such as biotechnology, lasers, robotics, fiber-optics, semiconductors, electronics and communications. High-tech stocks generally command higher P/E ratios and exhibit volatile earnings growth and stock price movements.

HISTORIC TRADING RANGES The price range within which a security has traded since going public. Other historical trading ranges include the 52-week range listed in the *Wall Street Journal* and the year's highs and lows as listed in stock guides such as *Standard and Poor's*.

HISTORIC YIELD The yield listed by money market and mutual funds. Usually computed by dividing the annual yield by a reasonable average.

HOLDER OF RECORD The investor whose name is registered as the security owner at the close of business on the record date set by the company. Entitlement to cash and stock dividends is determined by the holder of record on that date.

HOLDING COMPANY A corporation that controls another company through ownership of sufficient stock to influence its board of directors. In order to report consolidated results and share the tax benefits of consolidation, a corporation must own at least 80 percent of the subsidiary's voting stock. Many banks and utilities have established holding companies to circumvent restrictions placed on their operations under federal securities legislation.

HOLDING PERIOD The period of time an investment is held by its owner. Previous to tax reform legislation, assets held less than six months were taxed as short term gains while assets held longer than six months were deemed capital gains and received favored tax treatment. Under current tax law, all gains from the sale of investments are taxed as ordinary income.

HOME EQUITY ACCOUNT A revolving credit line secured by a second mortgage allowing homeowners to tap the appreciated value of their home. The home equity account makes borrowing against a house easy since the loan takes the form of a check written against the home equity account. Benefits include lower interest rates, tax advantages, and convenient borrowing.

HORIZONTAL PRICE MOVEMENT The charted price movement of a security that displays a narrow price range over an extended period of time. Also pertains to a flat market with very little price movement. See *Horizontal Price Movement* in Section II for a chart example and further explanation.

HORIZONTAL SPREAD An option trading strategy involving purchase and sale of the same number of option contracts with the same exercise price, but with differing expiration dates. Sometimes denoted as a calendar spread due to the different expiration dates. For example, an investor might purchase call options in XYZ, Inc. at a striking price of 10 with expiration dates of May and August. The investor would buy both periods because of not being positive of the time frame in which Armco Inc. is expected to rise above 10.

HOT ISSUE A newly issued security that is in great demand by the investing public resulting in rapid price rise after the initial offering. For over-the-counter stocks, an OTC bid over the issue price on the day the security is offered for sale results in special NASD (National Association of Securities Dealers) rules being placed in effect for the hot issue.

HOUSE CALL A notification from the brokerage house that a customer's margin account equity is below the required maintenance level. The customer must provide additional cash or securities to the margin account or the broker will be forced to liquidate the customer's position to satisfy the deficiency. Margin requirement minimums are set by Regulation T of the Federal Reserve Board. In addition, brokerage houses may set additional margin requirements. See *House Maintenance Requirements* in Section I and *Margin* in Section II.

HOUSE MAINTENANCE REQUIREMENTS Brokerage house policy setting the minimum equity level for customer margin accounts. If a customer's equity falls below this minimum requirement, the broker must request the client to supply additional equity in the form of cash and/or securities. Should the client fail to meet the house call for additional equity, the broker will liquidate the customer's position to satisfy the margin requirements. House maintenance requirements set by brokerage houses are generally higher than those required by the securities industry self-regulatory bodies and the Federal Reserve Board's Regulation T. See *House Call* in Sections I and II.

HOUSE RULES A brokerage house's internal policies and procedures regulating the opening and handling of customer accounts. To insure compliance with industry and governmental requirements, house rules are usually more restrictive.

HOUSING STARTS A leading indicator of the U.S. economic condition. An increase or decrease in the number of housing starts has a ripple effect through many other industries: construction financing, mortgage banking, construction, home appliances, building products, utilities, and home services. See *Indicator* in Sections I and II.

HYBRID ANNUITY An investment contract sold by insurance companies that provides the investor with features of both fixed and variable annuities. The investor can choose the percentage of the investment that will be invested in a fixed annuity with a guaranteed rate of return and the percentage to be invested in a variable annuity with a potential for higher gains with more risk. See *Annuity* in Sections I and II.

HYPOTHECATION The pledging of securities by a customer to the broker to cover purchases of other securities or to cover short sales. Ownership of the securities is maintained by the investor while the securities serve as collateral. The written agreement signed by the client that allows the shares to be used as collateral is known as the hypothecation agreement. Should the broker use the same securities as collateral for a broker's loan with a financing institution, the process is termed rehypothecation. See *Rehypothecation* in Section I.

I

ILLIQUID A security without an active secondary market making it hard for the owner of the security to sell his position to raise cash. Any investment that is not easily convertible into cash. For example, antique cars, paintings, and stamp collections may require a long period of time to effect a sale at favorable prices. See *Liquidity* in Section I.

IMBALANCE OF ORDERS A significant oversupply of either buy or sell orders in relation to each other. The imbalance may be the result of a major news event affecting the security such as takeover rumors, major mineral find or technological breakthrough, announced stock split or significantly higher or lower earnings results. The order imbalance hampers the orderly market process and trading may be suspended in the stock until sufficient offsetting orders are placed to correct the imbalance.

IMMEDIATE-OR-CANCEL ORDER An investor limit order requiring the broker to purchase or sell as much of the order that can be executed as soon as the bid or offer is entered. Any part of the order not immediately executed is automatically canceled.

Brokers usually handle immediate-or-cancel orders in significant quantities.

IMMEDIATE PAYMENT ANNUITY An annuity purchased with a single payment requiring annuity payments to begin immediately. Usually, monthly payments continue for the life of the annuity holder or for a predetermined number of years as elected by the purchaser. See *Annuity* in Sections I and II.

IMMUNIZATION The investment strategy of protecting an investment portfolio against interest rate risk by attempting to cancel out its two components, price risk and reinvestment risk.

INACTIVE BOND CROWD Term denoting New York Stock Exchange bonds that trade infrequently. Buy and sell orders for inactive bonds are stored in metal storage racks pending execution or cancellation. Also called cabinet crowd due to the metal storage cabinets. See *Convertible* in Section II for discussion of investment strategy.

INACTIVE SECURITY A stock or bond with little active secondary market following. See *Illiquid* in Section I.

IN-AND-OUT TRADER An investor who buys and sells the same security position in the same trading day in order to gain from intra-day market price changes.

INCOME BOND Generally a bond issued by a company reorganizing under bankruptcy regulations where interest is paid only if the company earns enough to cover interest charges. Income bonds trade flat without accrued interest. See *Flat Bond* in Section I.

INCOME INVESTMENT COMPANY Investment management company whose mutual fund's primary investment goal is to maximize income for fund participants. In contrast to growth funds, the income investment company invests in high-yield stocks and bonds versus growth stocks. See *Growth Fund* in Section I.

INCOME LIMITED PARTNERSHIP Limited partnership geared to generating high income from real estate, oil and gas, movie investments, and equipment leasing. Generally the high income is tax sheltered by the use of IRA's, Keogh plans or pension funds.

INDENTURE The legal contract specifying the terms and conditions between a bond issuer and the bondholders. Included in the indenture are repayment provisions, call or redemption terms, bond forms, collateral, sinking fund provisions and working capital and/or current ratio restrictions. Usually, the corporation's bank or trust company serves as trustee for the bond issue. See *Calls* in Section I.

INDEPENDENT BROKER OR $2 BROKER Member of the New York Stock Exchange who executes orders on the floor of the exchange for other members having more volume than they can handle at a particular time. They also execute orders for firms who do not have their own exchange member on the floor. Originally called $2 brokers because their round lot commission was fixed. Now commissions between independent brokers and commission brokers are negotiated.

INDEX Statistical measurements used in evaluating changes in the economy and financial and commodity markets. Stock exchange indexes reflect composite market prices and the number of shares outstanding for corporations in the index. Major stock indexes include Dow Jones Industrial Average, New York Stock Exchange Index, Value Line Index, Wilshire 5000, Standard and Poor's Index, and Barron's Group Stock Averages. The indexes provide a broad measurement of market trends. See *Stock Indexes* in Sections I and II.

INDEX FUND A mutual fund portfolio holding securities that comprise one of the major indexes such as The Standard & Poor 500. Proponents of index funds believe that index funds will perform as well as the general market without undue financial risk. Buying shares in an index fund or constructing a portfolio to resemble a broad-based index is termed indexing.

INDICATED YIELD The yield determined by dividing the coupon or dividend rate by the current market value of the security. See *Current Yield* in Section I.

INDICATION The approximate trading price range for a stock which has had trading in the securities halted due to an imbalance of orders. See *Imbalance of Orders* in Section I.

INDICATOR A measurement of the U.S. economy or securities markets used by economists and investment analysts to predict future economic and financial events. Examples of indicators are housing starts, interest rate changes, utility consumption, railcar loadings, and cardboard box production. Some indicators precede economic events and are termed leading indicators, while others follow economic events and are called lagging indicators. See *Indicator* in Section II for a discussion of major indicators and see *Leading Indicator* in Section I.

INDIVIDUAL RETIREMENT ACCOUNT (IRA) A tax-deferred personal retirement account in which an employed individual and spouse may deposit up to $2,000 a year ($2,250 including a non-working spousal deposit and $4,000 if both persons are working). For a couple filing jointly, the maximum

$2,000 deduction for each spouse is phased out if adjusted gross income (AGI) is between $40,000-$50,000. No deduction is allowed if AGI is $50,000 or more. Prior to recent tax changes, all working people were allowed a tax deduction for IRA contributions. Now more stringent eligibility tests must be passed to permit a tax deduction from taxable income.

IRA portfolios may be invested in various financial vehicles: stocks, bonds, certificates of deposit, mutual funds, money market accounts, etc.

Refer to *IRA* in Section II for IRA contribution tax deduction requirements and a discussion of IRA benefits.

INITIAL MARGIN The amount of equity which a customer must deposit with a broker prior to making a margin transaction. The broker furnishes the balance, charging margin interest rates. Minimum margin requirements are set by the Federal Reserve Board under Regulation T but many brokerage firms have stricter margin requirements. See *Margin* and *Maintenance Margin* in Section I.

IPO (Initial Public Offering) A corporation's first public offering of stock, usually underwritten by a single investment banker or a pool of investment bankers and brokerage firms. Depending on market circumstances and the individual firm's financial expertise, a firm may attempt its offering directly to the public.

INSIDE INFORMATION Material information not known by the general public that would influence the price of the affected company's stock. Examples would be takeover information, favorable or unfavorable news relating to company earnings or operations, and dividend or stock split information. SEC regulations forbid persons with inside information to trade in the stock for their personal benefit. The 1980s experienced a substantial increase in insider trading investigations, indictments and convictions. A more clear definition of insider trading should be formulated as criminal insider cases are adjudicated. See *Insider* in Section I.

INSIDE MARKET Also called the wholesale market, the inside market is where dealer-brokers trade with each other for their own account. Typically, the spread between bid and asked prices in the inside market is smaller than in the outside or retail market.

INSIDER Anyone having access to material corporate information. Generally used to indicate corporate officers and board of directors. SEC regulations prohibit the trading by those possessing inside information. See *Inside Information* in Section I.

INSTITUTION BROKER A broker who services the security transactions for major investor institutions such as banks, insurance companies, mutual funds, health and welfare and pension funds, and trust institutions.

INSTITUTIONAL INVESTOR Investor organizations that trade large volumes of securities thereby commanding reduced commissions and other special treatment. A substantial portion of daily trading is for the account of institutional investors such as banks, trusts, pension funds, insurance companies, and mutual funds.

INSURED ACCOUNT As related to securities transactions, brokerage accounts are insured by the SIPC (Securities Investor Protection Corporation). Total coverage is $500,000 per account. Cash coverage is limited to $100,000 per account. Some brokerage firms provide additional insurance for their customers backed by blanket bonds. See *Securities Investor Protection Corporation (SIPC)* in Section I.

INTERCOMMODITY SPREAD A commodity trading technique where an investor attempts to profit from the price relationship between related commodities by maintaining a long position in one commodity and a short position in a related commodity.

INTERDELIVERY SPREAD A trading strategy where an investor attempts to profit from the price difference fluctuations by simultaneously purchasing a contract for one month and selling the same contract in another month.

IN THE MONEY An option is said to be in the money if the current market price is higher than the striking price of a call option or lower than the striking price of a put option. See *Striking Price* and *Intrinsic Value* in Section I.

INTRINSIC VALUE The difference between the current market price of the underlying security and the striking price of a related option. When the intrinsic value is positive, the option is said to be in the money. For instance, when ABC, Inc. call options traded at 12 1/2 and the stock traded at 13 3/8 the calls had intrinsic value of 7/8 and were in the money. For a put to have intrinsic value, the current market price of the underlying security must be below the striking price. If the intrinsic value is negative, the call is said to be out of the money or at the money. See *In The Money* and *Out Of The Money* in Section I.

INVESTMENT BANKER Firm specializing in the sale and underwriting of new securities to the public.

INVESTMENT COMPANY A financial organization that sells shares in itself to the public in order to invest in a portfolio of securities.

INVESTMENT CLUB An investment club is a partnership of investors pooling their resources to make security purchases based on a consensus of opinion. Club rules stipulate the amount of money which must be invested by individual members each period, how security purchase and sale decisions are made, etc. The National Association of Investors Corporation helps clubs get organized and provides a monthly investing magazine for member clubs. The NAIC is located at 711 West Thirteen Mile Road, Madison Heights, Michigan 48071. The American Association of Individual Investors, 625 North Michigan Avenue, Chicago, Illinois 60611, assists individuals in investment study. See *Investment Club* in Section II for a discussion of club membership benefits.

INVESTMENT VALUE The straight-debt value of a convertible bond.

J

JOINT BOND A bond which has its principal and interest payments guaranteed by someone other than the issuer. See *Guaranteed Bond* in Section I.

JUNIOR OBLIGATION A debt or equity security with lower payment rights compared to other company securities. The indenture specifies a specific issue's rank in the hierarchy, repayment or conversion privileges. Preferred stocks are junior obligations to corporate bonds. Bond obligations may be junior to other debt such as commercial paper, credit lines, and promissory notes.

JUNK BONDS A term used to describe bonds with investment ratings lower than BB by both Standard & Poor's and Fitch and Ba2 by Moody's. These bonds are highly speculative and accordingly carry higher interest rates. Institutions with fiduciary responsibilities are prevented from owning junk bonds. Several studies have shown that junk bond returns can outperform the market. Junk bond funds attempt to spread the risk while earning a higher yield.

K

KEOGH PLAN A tax-deferred investment retirement plan that allows self-employed persons to deposit money for themselves and their employees annually tax-free. All investment income accumulates tax-deferred until capital is withdrawn. Like IRA's, Keogh plans allow the purchase of a number of financial investments.

KICKER Special features of a debt obligation added to promote marketability. Convertible provisions at specific prices provide interest income with the possibility of cashing in on gains in the underlying stock price. Rights and warrants are two popular equity kickers.

L

LAPSED OPTION An option that was not exercised prior to its expiration and is now worthless.

LAST SALE Term describing the most recent transaction of a particular security. It is not the same as the close which is the final trade of a security for the day. SEC regulations specify that short sales may be made on an uptick, at a price higher than the last sale, or at the same price of the last sale if the last sale price was higher than the preceding transaction. See *Uptick* in Section I.

LAST TRADING DAY The day when a futures contract must be settled either by an offsetting transaction or physical delivery of the commodity. In reality, most futures contracts are offset, but one farmer recently made a physical delivery since it was cheaper than the offsetting transaction.

LAST TAPE Technical condition delaying the display of price changes of trading on the stock exchange. Generally, the first digit of a stock price will be dropped when there is a tape delay. For example a sale of ABC stock at a price of 34 1/2 will show on the tape as 4 1/2.

LEADING INDICATOR A measurement of the U.S. economy or securities markets. Leading indicators tend to accurately predict rises and declines in the business cycle. Computed by the U.S. Department of Commerce's Bureau of Economic Analysis, the indictors are watched closely by economists, investors, the Federal Reserve Board, and financial institutions. See *Indicator* in Section I for further discussion and Section II for a listing of leading indicators.

LENDING AT A PREMIUM The situation that occurs when a security is in heavy demand making it difficult to borrow for a short sale. A fee is imposed for the borrowed securities needed to effect the short sale. Normally short sale stock borrowings are loaned flat, that is, without a fee or premium. See *Loaned Flat* in Section I.

LEVERAGE The use of non-owned capital to increase the amount of a security that can be purchased. Margin, option, rights and warrants are all methods of obtaining leverage.

LIMIT The amount a commodity is permitted to decline or advance during a day's trading, measured from the commodity's previous day settlement price.

LIMIT ORDER A security transaction order to buy or sell a specific security at a specified price or for a specified time. A limit order may be placed to purchase 500 shares of ZZZ Corporation at $12 or better. If the current market price is $13 the limit order will not be executed until the ZZZ stock price drops to $12 or less. A fill or kill limit order specifics that the broker cancel the order if it cannot be executed immediately.

LIQUIDITY The ease at which financial assets can be converted to cash without creating a substantial change in price or value. Liquidity is influenced by the amount of float in the security, investor interest, and size of the investment being converted to cash. See *Acid-test* and *Current Ratio* in Section I for a discussion of measuring a firm's liquidity.

LISTED OPTION Put or call options traded on a registered exchange.

LISTED STOCK Stock or bond securities that have met the listing requirements of the particular stock exchange and are actively traded on that exchange. Typical requirements include demonstrated earning power, asset valuation, broad distribution of stock and minimum market value. Unlisted stocks are traded over-the-counter. Generally, listing provides liquidity, an orderly market and price spreads, protective regulations, financial information requirements, and higher collateral value for loan purposes.

Stock exchanges and the SEC have rules for suspension of trading and delisting.

LOAD FUND Mutual funds with sales charges. Mutual funds without sales charges (load fees) are termed no-load funds.

LOANED FLAT The loaning of securities to cover short positions without a charge or premium. See *Lending At Premium* in Section I.

LOCKED MARKET A condition in a highly competitive market when the bid and offer prices for a security are the same. After the offsetting purchases and sales are completed and additional buyers and sellers enter, the market unlocks.

M

M1 The standard measure of money supply comprised of currency, demand deposits and other checkable deposits.

M2 M1 plus savings and small time deposits, money market deposit accounts and shares in money market funds.

M3 M2 plus large time deposits.

MAINTENANCE MARGIN The minimum equity value that must be maintained in a margin account. Regulation T requires a deposit of $2,000 before any credit can be extended. Initial margin requirements of 50% of the market value of margined positions must be maintained. Individual brokerage houses generally have tighter margin requirements called house maintenance requirements. When the market value of margined securities drops below the minimum margin percent, a margin call is sent to the customer requesting additional cash or securities as collateral. See *House Call* and *House Maintenance Requirements* in Section I.

MANAGED ACCOUNT An investment account where the investor has turned over direction of the account to a professional manager. Investment advisory firms and trust departments handle managed accounts for a management fee, generally a percentage of asset valuation.

MARGIN The equity an investor deposits with the broker to borrow additional funds to purchase securities. The initial margin is set by regulation. Maintenance margin is the minimum acceptable percentage difference between the underlying security's current market value and the amount borrowed from the broker. The account where margin transactions are carried out is called a margin account. See *Maintenance Margin* and *House Maintenance Requirements* in Section I, and *Margin* in Section II.

MARGIN CALL A demand from the broker for additional cash or securities to bring the margin account back within minimum maintenance limits. See *House Call* in Section I.

MARGIN AGREEMENT The written agreement signed by the client that details how the broker loans money or stock to a customer. See *Hypothecation* in Section I.

MARKET BREADTH The percentage of stocks involved in a market move. A market move with good breadth signals strength and a longer-lasting move. Market breadth can be monitored by the advance/decline statistics published in major investment publications.

MARKET IF TOUCHED ORDER (MIT) A transaction order specifying to buy when the commodity reaches the specified price; the MIT order then becomes a market order to be executed at the best possible available price.

MARKET MAKER The dealer in the over-the-counter market who maintains firm bid and offer prices for a specific security by being willing to buy or sell a round lot of the security. The market maker performs the same functions in the over-the-counter market that a specialist performs on the exchange.

MARKET ORDER An order specifying to purchase or sell at the best possible price when the order reaches the trading floor. The broker must purchase at the lowest price available or sell at the highest price available immediately. See *At the Market* in Section I.

MARKET PRICE The last reported sales price on an exchange and the average of bid and asked prices in the over-the-counter market.

MARKET TIMING An investment strategy based on evaluation of such factors as technical indicators, interest rates, market direction and strength, and other economic factors. The strategy attempts to time purchases and sales of securities to maximize investment return.

MARKET TONE The health and vitality of the market. Market tone is positive when dealers and market makers trade actively on narrow bid and offer spreads. Market tone is negative when trading spreads widen and trading is inactive.

MARK TO THE MARKET The process of debiting and crediting gains and losses resulting in changes in market prices of the underlying securities. Mark to the market is used in short sale and margin accounts.

MAY DAY On May 1, 1975, fixed minimum brokerage commissions were ended allowing brokerage firms to set their own commission rate schedules. See *Discount Broker* in Section I.

MINUS TICK The sale of a security at a price lower than the previous sale. Also called downtick.

MONEY MARKET The market for short-term, liquid, low risk securities such as negotiable certificates of deposit, treasury bills, and commercial paper.

MONTHLY INVESTMENT PLAN The strategy of building a portfolio through periodic investments in a specific security or group of securities. In theory, the investor benefits from dollar cost averaging. Investment clubs are good vehicles for monthly investment strategies.

MORAL OBLIGATION BOND Municipal bonds authorized by the state legislature which do not carry a legal obligation to repay the debt but are backed by the moral obligation of the issuing body.

MOVING AVERAGE An investment strategy used by chartists and technicians to plot the price direction of a specific security, group of stocks, commodities or the general market. As a new price is added to the average, the oldest price drops off. See *Moving Average* in Section II for an illustrated example.

MUTUAL FUNDS An investment company that sells shares in itself to the public and uses the proceeds to purchase common stocks, bonds, and/or money market securities. The mutual fund offers diversification, professional management, and liquidity. Mutual funds can be tailored to any investment philosophy. Gold funds, junk bond funds, convertible funds, and growth funds are some examples.

N

NAKED OPTION Any option that the buyer or seller does not have covered with an underlying security position. For example, a writer of a call option that does not own the underlying stock is writing a naked call option. Similarly, a writer of a put option without a corresponding short position in the underlying stock is writing a naked put option. Naked options are used to gain substantial leverage. See *Call Options* in Sections I and II for further discussion and examples.

NASD (NATIONAL ASSOCIATION OF SECURITIES DEALERS) The self-regulating body of brokers and dealers overseeing over the counter trading practices. The Board of Governors, assisted by committees, draws up rules for fair conduct to maintain high standards in investment dealings. Violation of NASD rules subjects the dealer or broker to disciplinary action including expulsion from membership. The SEC has the power to review all NASD disciplinary actions.

NASDAQ National Association of Securities Dealers Automated Quotation system owned by the Nation Association of Securities Dealers (NASD). The system provides computerized quotes of market makers for stocks traded over the counter.

NATIONAL ASSOCIATION OF INVESTORS CORPORATION An association established in 1951 to help with the establishment of investment clubs. The association provides guidelines, a monthly investment publication, stock study materials, and representation with government agencies as a trade association. Individual members not belonging to an investment club can participate in a separate monthly investment plan. The association is located at 711 West Thirteen Mile Road, Madison Heights, Michigan 48071. See *Investment Club* in Sections I and II.

NATIONAL QUOTATION BUREAU The chief source of quotations for the over-the-counter market in stocks and bonds. Offered on a subscription basis, the National Quotation Bureau distributes stock quotes (pink sheets) and bond quotes (yellow sheets) along with a list of firms wishing to trade them. See *Pink Sheets* and *Yellow Sheets* in Section I.

NEGATIVE YIELD CURVE An abnormal condition in investment markets when short-term interest rates are higher than long-term rates. Since lenders who loan their money for longer periods are susceptible to more risk, long-term interest rates are generally higher to compensate for the additional risk. A negative yield curve situation may arise after a period of relatively high rates. Lenders become reluctant to commit to longer terms at the current high rates and subsequently yields begin to rise on short-term loads, eventually surpassing yields on long-term loans, thereby creating the negative yield curve. See *Negative Yield Curve* in Section II for an illustration.

NEGOTIABLE Possessing the ability to have title transferred from one owner to another. A negotiable security can be endorsed over or assigned to another investor.

NET ASSET VALUE (NAV) The quoted market value of a mutual fund share. Net asset value is calculated after the close of the market each day by taking the closing market value of all securities owned plus all other assets less all liabilities and dividing the result by the total number of shares outstanding.

NET CHANGE The difference in closing trading prices from one day to the next. For over-the-counter securities, it is the change between bid prices from one day to the next.

NO-LOAD FUND Mutual fund that does not charge a sales (load) fee.

NOMINAL INTEREST RATE The stated interest rate on a financial instrument.

NOMINAL QUOTATION Bid and ask quotes supplied by a market maker for valuation purposes only. The market maker is not required to trade at nominal quotation prices but NASD rules require nominal quotes to be specifically identified as such.

NOMINAL YIELD The annual interest paid by a security divided by the par value of the security. Depending on current interest rates, the nominal yield may be substantially higher or lower than current yield. The nominal yield of a $1,000 bond that pays $95 in interest annually is 9.5% (95/1,000). See *Current Yield* in Section I.

NONCALLABLE A bond or preferred stock which cannot be called for redemption by the issuer before maturity for bonds or for the lifetime of the issue for preferred stocks. Securities may be noncallable for a number of years and thereafter be callable under specific conditions. Callable terms are spelled out in the indenture or prospectus.

NONCUMULATIVE PREFERRED STOCK A preferred stock class that does not accumulate unpaid dividends. If the board votes not to pay dividends in a given year, the dividends cannot be carried forward to be paid in another year. See *Cumulative Preferred Stock* in Section I.

NONPARTICIPATING PREFERRED STOCK A preferred stock with a specified dividend which cannot be changed. The nonparticipating preferred stockholder will not be able to share in any additional earnings distributions. Most preferred stock is nonparticipating. See *Participating Preferred Stock* in Section I.

NONREFUNDABLE A bond that the issuer is prevented from retiring with the proceeds of a subsequent issue. The nonrefundable provision may be permanent or restricted to refunding at specific future dates or at specific interest rates.

NO-PAR STOCK Stock without face value. The major advantage to a company issuing no-par stock is price flexibility. The issue may be sold at any price and the value for balance sheet purposes may be fixed by the Board of Directors. The proceeds may be carried as capital stock or capital surplus or split between the two capital accounts.

NOT HELD (NH) A market order instruction allowing the floor broker latitude in time and/or price in executing the best possible purchase or sale. The floor broker is not held accountable if the order is not executed at the best terms available.

NR (NOT RATED) Symbol used by ratings services indicating a security has not been rated. There is neither a negative or positive implication by the NR symbol.

O

ODD-BALL THEORIES Investment theories not readily explained by rational investment behavior or techniques but with proven track records of price movements coincidentally related to events external to the stock market and the investing world. See *Odd-Ball Theories* in Section II.

ODD-LOT Any securities trade made in less than round lot (100 share) multiples. Brokers charge higher commissions for executing odd lot transactions. See *Differential* and *Round Lot* in Section I.

ODD-LOT THEORY Investment strategy based on the belief that small investors who conduct odd-lot transactions are generally wrong in market timing and direction. Odd-lot theory states that strong odd-lot buying in a rising market is a sign of weakness and signals a retreat in the future. Likewise, an increase of odd-lot selling in a declining market is a sign of strength and signals a potential recovery.

OFFER The lowest price at which a dealer or seller is willing to accept, also called asked price. Bid is the highest price a dealer or buyer is willing to pay. The difference between bid and offer (asked) is called the price spread.

OFFSET A securities transaction that replaces or reverses a future position nearing maturity. A hedge designed to protect a gain or price.

OPEN A purchase or sale order that has not been executed. See *Good-Till-Canceled Order* in Section I.

OPEN-ENDED CD A flexible certificate of deposit which allows periodic deposits over its life. A major benefit to open-ended CD holders is the ability to deposit additional money that will earn the specified rate even though interest rates have declined on other instruments and new CD's.

OPEN-END INVESTMENT COMPANY An investment company whose capitalization changes as new shares are sold and outstanding shares are redeemed. The price is determined by net asset value. If sales charges are imposed, the fund is termed a load fund. Conversely, if no sales fee (load) is charged, the fund is no-load. See *Net Asset Value* and *Closed-End Fund* in Section I.

OPTION A security that provides the right to purchase or sell a specified number of shares of a particular stock at a fixed price for a specified time limit. If the option is not exercised before the expiration date, all monies paid for the option are forfeited. A call option is a contract giving the holder the right to buy the underlying security at a specific price during a specified period of time. See *Call Option* and *Put Option* in Sections I and II. See *Option* in Section II for a glossary of option terms.

OPTION AGREEMENT The contract signed by an investor when opening an option trading account. The agreement details customer financial information, verifies receipt of the option prospectus, and confirms the customer's willingness to follow options trading rules and regulations.

OPTION HOLDER An investor who has purchased a put or call option which has not yet been exercised or resold.

OPTION PREMIUM The amount per share paid by the option purchaser for the right to purchase shares in the case of a call and the right to sell shares in the case of a put at a specific price within a specified time frame. Option premiums are listed in 8ths or 16ths in option quotation tables. For example An option trading at 3/8 sells at a premium of 37.5 cents a share or $37.50 for the 100 share option. All options are for increments of 100 share blocks.

OPTION SPREAD An option strategy involving the purchase and sale of options within the same class simultaneously in order to capitalize on the narrowing or widening of the spread between the particular options. The option spread strategy can be utilized in both rising and declining markets. An investor who holds an August 15 call and writes a November 20 call has a call spread.

OPTION WRITER Any person or organization that sells puts and calls in order to earn the option premium paid by the purchaser. A call option writer guarantees to the holder that the writer will sell 100 shares of underlying stock per option at a specific price for a specified period of time. A put option writer guarantees to the holder that the writer will purchase 100 shares of the underlying stock per option at a specific price for a specified period of time. In return for providing the option guarantee, the writer earns a fee called the option premium. For example, a writer of an XYZ September 12 1/2 option at $1 guarantees the holder the right to purchase 100 shares of XYZ stock for $12 1/2 share until the September 15 expiration date. The writer earns a $100 premium ($1 x 100 shares) for writing this call option.

OPTIONAL CALL A bond or preferred stock redemption option that allows the issuer to call the bond before maturity date or call the stock at market price plus a specified premium.

OR BETTER (OB) A limit order directing the broker to purchase or sell securities at a specified price or better.

ORIGINAL ISSUE DISCOUNT BOND A bond issue that is offered at a discount from par value by the original underwriter in the primary market. The discount is usually offered to attract investors to bond issues with coupon rates lower than current market rates. Zero coupon bonds are examples of original issue discount bonds that are attractive investments for IRA's.

OUT OF THE MONEY An option is said to be out of the money if the current market price is lower than the striking price of a call option or higher than the striking price of a put option. An out of the money option may still have some value due to the possibility that the underlying stock price will move prior to expiration of the option. See *Intrinsic Value, In The Money* and *Striking Price* in Section I.

OVER THE COUNTER (OTC) A securities market not conducted through a formal exchange. Over the counter securities are traded via a telephone and computerized network linking over the counter security dealers. The National Association of Securities Dealers (NASD) oversees over the counter transactions and regulations. See *National Association of Securities Dealers* in Section I.

P

PAR VALUE The value assigned to a security upon issuance. For bonds and preferred stock, par value is equivalent to face value. Common stock par value is assigned arbitrarily and is of little significance. See *Face Value* in Section I.

PARITY Situation when the value of the underlying security equals the market value of the convertible security. For example, parity exists if a bond is convertible into 25 shares of common stock and the bond currently sells for $1,000 and the stock sells for $40 a share.

PARTICIPATING PREFERRED STOCK A preferred stock paying a specified dividend but which also shares or participates in any additional earnings distributions to shareholders. Most preferred stocks are nonparticipating. An example of a participating preferred stock is one with a specified dividend of $2.50 a share but which will share in additional earnings distributions up to $1.00 a share. See *Nonparticipating Preferred Stock* in Section I.

PASSED DIVIDEND An anticipated dividend on stock which is not declared by the board of directors. A passed dividend on common shares does not have to be made up by the company. In contrast, a passed dividend on cumulative preferred shares must be accrued and paid before any common stock dividends can be paid. See *Cumulative Preferred* in Section I.

PAYDOWN The refunding of an outstanding bond issue via the floating of a smaller debt issue. For example, a company can paydown a $50 million outstanding debt issue with a high interest rate of 15% with a smaller bond issue of $40 million yielding 10%.

PAYMENT DATE Date on which a dividend or interest payment will be made in cash.

PAYOUT RATIO A stock performance measurement signifying the percentage of a company's profit paid out as dividends to common shareholders. Typically, growth companies retain earnings to spur further growth, while old line companies, banks, and utilities tend to have higher payout ratios.

PENNANT A stock or commodity stock pattern outlining a pointed flag or pennant facing to the right. The pennant figure forms as the peaks and valleys become less pronounced, usually on reduced trading volume. Like its flag pattern counterpart, pennants are followed by steep price advances or declines. See *Flag* in Section I.

PENNY STOCKS Originally stocks selling for less than $1 a share. Inflation has taken its toll and penny stocks now refer to highly speculative stocks selling for up to $10 a share. Most penny stocks are traded over the counter or on smaller regional exchanges. Natural resource firms such as gold mining and oil exploration companies have traditionally used the penny stock market to raise capital. Today, many high-tech computer and biotechnology companies are first issued as penny stocks. See *Pink Sheet Stocks* in Section I. See *Penny Stocks* in Section II for penny stock trading strategies.

PERFORMANCE FUND An investment company mutual fund which invests its portfolio in high growth companies paying little or no dividends. The strategy is to share in above-average growth and stock returns rather than depend on dividend yield to earn acceptable earnings.

PERFORMANCE STOCK Company whose earnings are projected to rise substantially above the performance of the market in general. A performance stock tends to reinvest its capital and earnings in assets to realize an above-average rate of return.

PERIODIC PAYMENT PLAN An investment plan offered by mutual funds requiring regular monthly or quarterly investments. The investor signs a contract specifying periodic payments over a 10-, 15-, or 20-year period. Most plans offer completion insurance and have asset withdrawal privileges over the contract life after completion of the pay-in requirements. Benefits to investors include a diversified portfolio, reinvestment privileges, and dollar cost averaging. See *Dollar Averaging* in Section I.

PERPENDICULAR SPREAD An option investment strategy involving options with the same expiration dates but different strike prices.

PINK SHEET STOCKS Over-the-counter stocks that are not routinely traded or in the NASDAQ listings. They are listed on pink sheets compiled by the National Quotations Bureau daily. The pink sheets contain bid and asked prices and market makers for these highly traded over-the-counter stocks. Thinly traded debt securities are listed on yellow sheets. See *National Quotation Bureau*, *Penny Stocks* and *Yellow Sheets* in Section I.

PLAN COMPLETION INSURANCE Decreasing term life insurance offered to investors in mutual fund periodic payment plans. The insurance provides assurance of the plan continuation should the investor die before completing the plan contract. See *Periodic Payment Plan* in Section I.

PLUS TICK The trade of a security at a higher price than the previous transaction for the same security. A ticker tape listing as 30+ indicates that XYZ traded on a plus tick, up from 29 7/8 or lower on the previous trade. See *Last Sale* and *Uptick* in Section I.

POINT A point indicates a movement of $1 in the market. For instance if XYZ moved up three points, the stock price rose $3.00 a share. In relation to bonds, a point is a 1% change in the par value of the bond in relation to the bond's market value.

POINT AND FIGURE CHART A stock or commodity charting technique used to project the rise or decline in security price movements. Xs indicate upward price movements while Os indicate downward price movements. Each time price direction changes, a new column is used to track movement. The resulting chart of Xs and Os reflect the security's ability to sustain an upward or downward price movement. See *Point And Figure Chart* in Section II for further discussion and an illustrative example.

PORTFOLIO The investment holdings of an individual investor, bank, trust company, fiduciary fund or investment company. Portfolios tend to consist of a variety of investment securities in order to minimize investment risk.

POSITIVE YIELD CURVE The normal situation when interest rates on longer-term securities are greater than that offered on shorter-term securities. The higher interest compensates the investor for the additional risk involved in investing for longer periods of time.

PREEMPTIVE RIGHT A privilege extended to existing stockholders allowing them to purchase shares of an upcoming issue in an amount proportional to their current holdings before the shares are offered to the general investing public. The preemptive rights are intended to protect the investor from dilution by maintaining the proportional share of ownership. Examples of preemptive rights are subscription warrants. The current stockholder can use the warrants to purchase additional shares or sell the warrants on the open market.

PREFERRED STOCK A class of stock on which a company must pay a dividend before any dividend can be paid on the company's common stock. In addition, preferred stock enjoys prior claim to company assets over common stock in the case of a bankruptcy. The dividend rate is generally fixed and the preferred stock that pays a $6.00 dividend will be listed in the stock table and stock listing books as XYZ Company $6.00 Pfd. A cumulative preferred stock accumulates any unpaid dividend for future payment before any distribution can be made to common stockholders. Cumulative preferred stocks are designated as XYZ Company $6.00 cm Pfd. in stock listings. Noncumulative preferred stock does not accumulate unpaid dividends; they cannot be carried forward to future years. See *Cumulative Preferred Stock* and *Noncumulative Preferred Stock* in Section I.

PREMIUM The amount by which the market value of a preferred stock or bond exceeds its face value or par. For options, the premium is the amount paid by the option buyer for the right to purchase or sell a security during a specified time frame.

PREMIUM INCOME The income earned by an investor who sells put or call options. The investor who sells put and call options in order to earn premium income is called a grantor. The investor who writes options on owned underlying stock is said to be writing a covered option. If the underlying stock is not owned, the investor is writing a naked option. See *Grantor* in Section I.

PRICE CONTINUITY The situation when prices exhibit a high degree of continuity in a series of transactions. High price continuity provides more liquidity in the event a position has to be sold out.

PRICE/EARNINGS RATIO One of the most frequently used measurements of a stock's relative value to other stocks and the market in general. The price/earnings ratio (PE) is determined by dividing the stock's market price by its earnings per common share. The PE expresses how much an investor is paying for a potential future stream of earnings.

A company whose common stocks sells for $30.00 a share and earned $2.00 a share has a PE of 15 ($30.00/$2.00). Generally companies with high PE's are high-tech, relatively young companies in fast growing industries such as biotechnology, electronics, etc. Many high PE stocks do not pay dividends, preferring to conserve cash for rapid expansion of the business.

On the other hand, low PE stocks offer higher yields and lower risk. Some exception to this rule may be cyclical stocks and stocks whose erratic earnings record will not support a higher PE.

Price/earnings ratios show wide fluctuations between stock market highs and lows as well as substantial differences in individual stocks due to such factors as growth prospects, company size, capitalization, earnings trend, financial strength, industry trend, and management strength. See *E/P Ratio* in Section I.

PRICE GAP See *Gap* in Section I.

PRICE SPREAD An options strategy utilized by investors to take advantage of the movement of option prices by simultaneously purchasing and selling two options on the same underlying security with the same expiration date but with different exercise prices. An example of an option price spread is the purchase of an ABC August 12 1/2 call and the sale of an ABC August 10 call.

PRIMARY DISTRIBUTION The first sale of a new bond or stock issue. All issues of bonds are primary distributions. See *Secondary Distribution* in Section I.

PRIMARY EARNINGS PER SHARE The amount of earnings per common share before taking into account the potential conversion of common stock equivalents. See *Common Stock Equivalents, Earnings Per Share, Dilution* and *Fully Diluted Earnings Per Share* in Section I.

PRIMARY MARKET The market for new security issues typically involving the use of investment bankers to float the issue. In recent times, more companies have handled their own security issues in the primary market. See *Secondary Market* in Section I.

PRINCIPAL AMOUNT The face amount of any debt security. Also called par value.

PRIVATE PLACEMENT The sale of an issue of securities directly to a few investors, typically institutional investors.

PROGRAM TRADING Computerized strategy used by institutional investors to effect simultaneous buy and sell transactions triggered by rising or falling prices in order to profit from price discrepancies between an index of stock futures or options and the market price of the underlying stocks.

PROSPECTUS The printed summary of the registration statement which the SEC requires the issuer to furnish to prospective investors. The prospectus contains material information about the security offering, the company lines of business, financial information, management, litigation, and operations. A preliminary prospectus is called a red herring.

PROXY The authorization or power of attorney signed by a stockholder assigning the right to vote the shares to another party. The company management mails proxy statements to registered stockholders prior to the annual stockholders' meetings. The statement contains a brief explanation of proposed management sponsored voting items along with the opportunity to vote for or against each individual issue or transfer the right to vote for the issues to company management or another party.

PUT OPTION A contract giving the holder the right to sell the underlying security at a specific price during a specified period of time. The exercise price of the option is called the "striking price." See *Call Option* in Section I and *Put Option* in Section II for further discussion and put investment strategies.

Q

QUALITATIVE ANALYSIS Security analysis that uses subjective judgement in evaluating securities based on nonfinancial information such as management expertise, cyclicality of industry, strength of research and development, and labor relations.

QUANTITATIVE ANALYSIS Security analysis that uses financial information derived from company balance sheets, income statements, and 10k's to make an informed investment decision. Examples of quantitative analysis include review of company financial ratios, the cost of capital asset valuation, and sales and earnings trends.

QUICK RATIO The quick ratio or acid-test ratio is used to measure liquidity. It is regarded as an improvement over the current ratio which includes inventory, usually not very liquid.

The quick ratio is stated as current assets less inventory divided by current liabilities. An alternative divides cash, marketable securities and accounts receivable by current liabilities.

Normally, a quick ratio of 1 to 1 is satisfactory. However, an interruption or slowdown of cash receipts could spell trouble. Conversely, a company with a high quick ratio may not be using its capital effectively and its cash-rich position may invite a takeover. See *Acid-test Ratio* in Section II for an example.

QUIET PERIOD Period of time when the issue is in registration and the company is precluded from making promotional statements.

QUOTE A quote or quotation is the highest bid and lowest offer available for a security. The difference between the bid and ask is termed the price spread. See *Ask, Bid* and *Spread* in Section I.

R

RANGE The high and low price extremes over which the security has traded over a specific period of time. *The Wall Street Journal, Investor's Business Daily,* and *Barron's* list the 52-week price range; Standard & Poor's tear sheets list the calendar year range; the company annual reports list fiscal year price ranges.

Analysis of price ranges can help determine price support levels (bottoms) and tops for specific securities in certain time frames. A push through a bottom or top could signal strong downward or upward momentum.

RATE OF RETURN The current yield of a security determined by dividing the annual cash flow by the purchase price.

RATING The result of the review of the credit worthiness of a firm. Rating services such as Moody's, Fitch, and Standard & Poor's evaluate a firm to determine the credit risk of investing in the firm's securities.

RATIO ANALYSIS A quantitative investment analysis technique used to compare a company relative to other investment opportunities and the market in general. Changes in ratios can help signal important changes in the direction of the company's fortunes. Examples of ratios include price/earnings, acid-test or quick, debt or equity, inventory turnover, and gross margin.

REALIZED YIELD The return actually earned on a bond as opposed to the yield at maturity.

RECORD DATE The date determining who is eligible for dividends issued by the company. A dividend is declared by the board to holders on the record date. Also called date of record.

REDEMPTION Repayment of the principal amount of debt security in order to retire the debt. Redemption privileges are spelled out in the bond indenture. Redemption can be made before or at maturity depending upon call privileges. See *Call* and *Indenture* in Section I.

RED HERRING Slang term for a preliminary prospectus derived from the red caveat printed on the prospectus cover See *Prospectus* in Section I.

REGISTERED SECURITY A security registered on the books of the company with the owner's name. A registered security needs to be properly endorsed before effective title can be transferred. In contrast, a bearer security is owned by the person possessing it. See *Bearer Security* in Section I.

REHYPOTHECATION The repledging of securities which were originally pledged by the investor to the broker to cover purchases of other securities or to cover short sales. Typically, pledge securities act as collateral for margin loans. Upon signing of the margin account agreement, the investor authorizes the broker to repledge or rehypothecate the securities as collateral for a bank loan to finance the customer's margin account. See *Hypothecation* in Section I.

REINVESTMENT RATE RISK The interest rate risk resulting from the uncertainty of the rate at which future interest and other investment cash flows can be reinvested.

RELATIVE STRENGTH The technical analysis technique which compares the ratio of a stock's price to a market index or other index. The ratios are plotted over time to form a graph of relative prices.

RESIDUAL SECURITY A security with the potential to dilute earnings on common stock. Examples of residual securities include convertible bonds, preferred stock, and rights and warrants. See *Common Stock Equivalents, Dilution, Earnings Per Share, Fully Diluted Earnings Per Share, Rights,* and *Warrants* in Section I.

RESISTANCE LEVEL The upper price level at which the stock price has trouble breaking through. As stock prices reach a resistance level, stock holders will sell in hopes of repurchasing the shares after the stock price falls from the resistance level. Plotting of stock prices will indicate potential resistance levels. The lower end of the price range is called the support level. See *Support Level* in Section I. Also see *Tops and Bottoms* in Section II for a more detailed discussion and resistance level chart.

RESTRICTED ACCOUNT A margin account where the actual margin is between the initial margin and the maintenance margin requirement. When an account is restricted, additional margin purchases are prohibited.

RETIREMENT The calling of debt securities or preferred stock. Securities may be retired through early redemption call privileges or through the floating of another security issue. See *Redemption* in Section I.

RETURN Financial analysis measurement used to evaluate investment alternatives for fixed income securities. The return is the current yield or coupon rate divided by the purchase price. See *Return* in Section II for a discussion of various return ratios such as return on equity, return on assets, and return on invested capital.

REVERSAL Technical analysis term describing a major shift in direction of an investment security or market index as evidenced by its chart. Reversals must be distinguished from short term price changes resulting from normal market activity. A true reversal signals a major sustained direction change. See *Reversal* in Section II for an example of a reversal chart.

REVERSE SPLIT The reduction of the number of shares outstanding accompanied by an increase in the par value of the shares. The total number of shares have the same market value before and after the reverse split. A company would effect a reverse split in order to raise the price at which its shares are trading. See also *Split* in Section I.

REWARD-TO-VARIABILITY RATIO A measure of portfolio performance calculated as the ratio of excess portfolio return (return less the risk-free rate) to risk as measured by the standard deviation. See *Risk-free Rate of Return* in Section I.

REWARD-TO-VOLATILITY RATIO A measure of portfolio performance calculated as the ratio of excess portfolio return (return less the risk-free rate) to risk as measured by beta. See *Beta* and *Risk-free Rate of Return* in Section I.

RIGHT A privilege granted by the corporation to existing stockholders allowing them to subscribe to shares of an upcoming issue before it is offered to the general investing public. The current shareholder can purchase new shares in proportion to number of shares currently owned in relation to total outstanding shares. A major advantage of rights is that the shares can be purchased at below market prices. Rights are short-term options allowing the holder to purchase a specified number of shares from the corporation at a specific subscription price.

The rights, also known as subscription rights, are transferable and may be sold to others. To act on the offer, the shareholder sends the rights and the required dollar amount to the company or his broker for execution. See *Common Stock Equivalents* in Section I.

RISK The financial uncertainty that the actual return on an investment will be different from the expected return. Factors of risk that can affect an investment include inflation or deflation, currency exchange, liquidity, default by borrower, and interest rate fluctuations.

RISK-AVERSE INVESTOR An investor who will not assume a given level of risk unless there is an expectation of adequate compensation. Investors generally seek investments with the least amount of risk. The greater the risk, the greater the return demanded.

RISK-FREE ASSET An asset with a certain expected rate of return and a zero variance of return.

RISK-FREE RATE OF RETURN The return on a riskless asset. For example, the rate of return on U.S. Treasury securities.

RISK PREMIUM The additional compensation demanded by investors, above the risk-free rate of return, for assuming additional risk. The higher the additional risk, the larger the risk premium.

RISK-SENSITIVE Investor decision-making process designed to reduce the potential for loss or a rate of return less than anticipated.

ROUND LOT The normal trading unit for a security. The size of the round lot can vary depending on the type of security and the price. Moderately priced stocks typically trade in round lots of 100 shares. For very inexpensive stocks round lots may be 500 or even 1,000 shares. A trade in other than round lot multiples is called an odd-lot rate and will incur additional trading costs. See *Differential* and *Odd Lot* in Section I.

ROUND TURN The cycle of opening and closing out a futures position. Commodity brokerage commissions are based on a round turn.

S

SALES CHARGE The fee charged by an investment company, mutual fund, or unit investment trust when shares or units are purchased. Generally the fee is a percentage of the dollar value of the purchase. Funds without sales charges are called no-load funds. See *Load Fund* and *No-load Fund* in Section I.

SAME-DAY SUBSTITUTION The purchase and sale on the same day of marginable securities with the same market value thereby avoiding a margin call or a credit to the special miscellaneous account. See *House Call*, *Margin Call* and *Special Miscellaneous Account* in Section I.

SAUCER Stock or commodity chart pattern resembling a saucer due to the formation of a bottom and subsequent price rise. See *Saucer* in Section II for a more detailed description and illustration.

SCALE Information pertaining to a new serial bond issue detailing scheduled maturity, the number of bonds, maturity date, coupon rate and the offering price of a specific scheduled maturity.

SCALE ORDER An uncommon order directing the broker to purchase or sell two or more lots of the same stock at designated price variations. For example, an investor might place an order to sell 3,000 shares of XYZ stock in segments of 1,000 shares at each half-point as the market rises from a specified price.

SCRIP The fractional shares of stock issued by a company during a stock dividend, spin-off, split-up or other scrip or cash to purchase full shares. In the case of the investor not wishing to purchase additional shares, the scrip may be sold.

SCRIPOPHILY The hobby of collecting scarce stock and bond certificates. Obsolete security certificates may have collector value and monetary value for a number of reasons. The intricate artwork, signatures of historical figures, and the economic history of the issue. Some collectors specialize, collecting only railroad or mining certificates. NASCA, a division of R.M. Smythe & Co., Inc., regularly holds scripophily auctions and will price your certificate for a moderate fee.

Sometimes certificates previously worthless except for collector value increase their financial value through a unique turn of historic events. In 1987, the USSR offered to redeem bonds originally issued by the Czar in the early 1900s. The action was taken to pave the way for Russia to tap Western financial markets in the future.

SECONDARY DISTRIBUTION The sale of a block of securities by the holder, typically an institution. See *Primary Distribution* in Section I.

SECONDARY MARKET The market where previously issued securities are traded, including the formal stock and bond exchanges and over-the-counter markets. See *Primary Market* in Section I.

SECTOR FUND Mutual fund that specializes in a particular industry sector such as transportation or mining stocks.

SECURITIES INVESTOR PROTECTION CORPORATION (SIPC) The nonprofit corporation which insures customer securities and cash in accounts of member brokerage firms. Customer accounts are insured up to $500,000 including a maximum $100,000 in cash.

SELLING CLIMAX Technical term describing a drastic plunge in security prices usually signaling the panic near the end of a bear market. Technicians interpret the selling climax as a buying opportunity in anticipation of the rally that will shortly follow the drop in prices. See *Selling Climax* in Section II for further discussion and an illustration.

SELL OUT The liquidation of a customer's account which has not been paid for in accordance with trading regulations. The broker executes the sell out at the best possible prices but the customer is liable to the broker for any losses incurred.

SELL PLUS Instruction to broker to execute the sell transaction only if the trading price in the specified security is higher than the last differently priced preceding trade.

SELL THE BOOK Instruction to the broker to sell as many shares as possible at the then-prevailing bid price.

SENIOR DEBT A debt security entitled to payment prior to junior or subordinate debt obligations. The status of the senior debt is specified in the debt contract in relation to other outstanding debt and equity.

SEPARATE CUSTOMER Relates to insurance coverage under the Securities Investor Protection Corporation (SIPC) program protecting customer securities and cash in accounts of member brokerage firms. The maximum protection afforded by SIPC pertains to each separate customer. A separate customer is distinguished by different types of ownership. For example, a personal account for an individual and a joint account for husband and wife are separate customer accounts even though the husband or wife may own the personal individual account. On the other hand, different types of accounts (margin, cash, short, money market) under the same ownership are treated as a single customer account. See *Securities Investor Protection Corporation* in Section I.

SEPARATION THEOREM The belief that the investment decision is separate from the financing decision. The investment decision involves determining the mix of assets in a given portfolio, while the financing decision involves allocation of investable funds between the risk-free assets and the risky assets. See *Risk-free Asset* in Section I.

SERIAL BOND Bonds that mature at specified stated intervals, imprinted with a sequential serial number at the time of issue.

SETTLEMENT DATE The date by which a securities transaction must be cleared or settled.

SETTLEMENT PRICE The final daily market price at which the futures clearinghouse clears all outstanding trades and settles accounts between clearing members. The settlement price and the last transaction price may be different.

SHELF RULE Permits qualified companies to file a short form registration for securities to be sold over a period of time or off the shelf under favorable conditions.

SHORT AGAINST THE BOX The act of selling short against a long position in the same stock. Technically, the stock is held in safekeeping by the broker or in the "box". The strategy is used to protect a gain in the long position without having to sell the underlying shares. See *Short Sale* in Section I.

SHORT COVERING The act of purchasing securities to offset securities borrowed for a short sale position. See *Short Sale* in Section I.

SHORT HEDGE A trading strategy that limits the risk of loss in an investment. The short against the box strategy protects an existing holding from decreasing in value via an offsetting rise in the short position.

SHORT INTEREST The number of shares of a stock that have been sold short but have not yet been covered. Short interest compilations are followed because the short interest represents dormant demand for a stock which may come to life if short sellers must cover their positions due to a marked rise in the stock's price. On the other side of the coin, the higher the short interest in a stock, the more negative investors are about the stock or the company's future earnings potential.

SHORT INTEREST RATIO Technical analysis tool used in evaluating market sentiment. The short interest ratio is calculated by dividing the total sales sold short by the average daily trading volume.

SHORT INTEREST THEORY Theory based on the assumption that a large short interest position in a stock is a prelude to higher prices for the stock. The rationale for the short interest theory is that the large short position must be covered in the future, thereby creating buying pressure and driving the stock price up.

SHORT POSITION The result of having borrowed shares of stock in order to make a short sale.

SHORT SALE The sale of a stock not owned in order to take advantage of an anticipated drop in the stock's price. A short sale can also be made to protect a long position; in this case, it is called short against the box. See *Short Against The Box* in Section I. See *Short Sale* in Section II for a more complete description of short selling and examples.

SHORT-SALE RULE Securities and Exchange Commission rule stipulating that short sales can only be made when the stock is rising. The following conditions permit short sales: (1) a sale on an uptick or plus tick; in other words, if the previous sale price was higher than the one preceding it; (2) if the previous price is unchanged but higher than the preceding different price transaction. See *Plus Tick* in Section I.

SHORT SQUEEZE Rapid price rise forcing investors holding short positions to buy securities in order to cut short their losses. This action drives the price up further, squeezing out other short traders substantially increasing their losses. See *Short Interest Theory* and *Short Sale* in Section I.

SILVER-INDEXED BOND Bond based on redemption at maturity with funds equal to the price of silver for a specified number of ounces or by physical delivery of a specified number of ounces of silver.

SINGLE-PURCHASE CONTRACT An annuity purchased with a lump-sum payment. The owner may elect either immediate payout or future payout.

SINKING FUND A segregated fund required by indenture provisions providing for the company to accumulate money annually for the retirement of portions of a bond issue.

SOFT MARKET Stock market condition consisting of an oversupply of stock and little demand. Trading is relatively inactive and selling pressure can cause sharp price declines.

SOVEREIGN RISK The additional risk assumed by investors with funds invested in foreign counties. Sovereign risk includes currency translation losses, default of foreign governments on debts, and appropriation of company assets by the foreign government.

SPECIALIST A registered member of a stock exchange charged with maintaining a fair and orderly market in specific securities by buying or selling for his own account. Specialists also act as brokers for other members.

SPECIAL MISCELLANEOUS ACCOUNT A memorandum account kept by the broker to determine the amount of excess funds in a customer's margin account. It enables the broker to get a quick reading on the customer's margin status and how close a customer may be to a margin call. Although there may be excess funds in the special miscellaneous account, the customer does not have full discretion in the use of those funds. Special miscellaneous account funds are generated by market value increases, security sale proceeds, cash or stock dividends, and deposits of cash or securities in response to margin calls. See *Same-day Substitution* in Section I.

SPECIAL SITUATION A security which is currently undervalued by the market and should have a substantial price rise when the market takes into account special circumstances. Special situations can be the result of a management change, strategic acquisition, major mineral deposit find, technological breakthrough, new product or industry turnaround.

SPECULATION Risk-taking in order to make a profit from the increase or decrease of a security's market price. Speculators do not care about the long-term fundamentals of a particular security but instead invest based on their analysis of the security's future stock price movement. Speculation profit is primarily generated by the volatility of stock prices. Speculators help provide market price continuity and liquidity.

SPIN-OFF The setting up of a subsidiary as a separate corporate entity through the issuance of shares in the subsidiary to shareowners of the parent company. Some spin-offs are effected through a leveraged buyout by the subsidiary's present management. See *Spin-off* in Section II.

SPLIT The change in the number of authorized and outstanding shares through an amendment to the corporation's charter. Shareholder's equity stays the same as a result of a corresponding change in the par value of all previous authorized shares. Dividends are also adjusted to reflect the stock split. Stock splits may take several forms. For instance, a 2-for-1 split doubles the number of authorized shares while a 3-for-1 split triples the number of authorized shares.

A 3-for-1 stock split of a security selling for $30 a share and paying dividends of $1.20 a share would become a $10 stock with a 40-cent dividend payment rate after the split.

Stock splits can go in any direction, but generally securities split up. A split down is also called a reverse split where the number of shares is reduced. See *Reverse Split* in Section I, and *Split* in Section II.

SPLIT RATING The occurrence of the major rating services assigning different ratings to the same security. See *Rating* in Section I.

SPOT COMMODITY A commodity transaction that is entered with the anticipation of actual delivery of the commodity. Futures contracts with current month expiration dates are also called spot commodities.

SPOT MARKET The market for immediate delivery rather than trading in commodity of financial futures which may or may not be physically delivered. Spot market deliveries generally are required by the same or the next business day. Trading of futures contracts with current month expiration dates is also termed spot market reading. See *Futures Contract* and *Futures Exchange* in Section I.

SPOT MONTH The month that a futures contract becomes deliverable.

SPOT PRICE The actual price quoted for a physical or financial commodity for immediate cash market delivery.

SPREAD The simultaneous sale and purchase of an equivalent option varying in only one condition such as time, maturity or price. See *Price Spread* in Section I.

Also, the difference between the price at which a security can be purchased and the price at which it can be sold. See *Asked Price, Bid Price* and *Range* in Section I.

STANDARD & POOR'S STOCK PRICE INDEX The S&P 500 index is composed of 400 industrial, 40 financial, 40 public utility and 20 transportation securities. It is a broad-based index designed to measure the value changes of 500 widely owned common stocks. The stocks are weighted to reflect differences in the number of outstanding shares. See *Stock Indexes* in Section II for a more complete discussion of stock indexes.

STANDARDIZED UNEXPECTED EARNINGS A variable utilized in common stock selection. The standardized unexpected earnings (SUE) is determined by subtracting expected earnings from actual earnings and dividing by the standard error of the regression equation used to estimate the expected earnings.

STOCK The certificates representing ownership in a corporation. See *Bond, Common Stock* and *Preferred Stock* in Section I.

STOCK DIVIDEND The payment of a dividend by a corporation through the issuance of shares instead of cash. Each shareholder would receive a pro rata share of the new issue. Corporations use stock dividends in order to conserve cash for operations.

STOCKHOLDER OF RECORD The shareowner whose name appears on the books of a corporation as of a particular date. The stockholder of record is entitled to receive the dividends and other distributions declared by the board. See *Record Date* in Section I.

STOCK INDEXES Statistical measurements used in evaluation changes in financial and commodity markets. Stock exchange indexes reflect composite market prices and the number of shares outstanding for corporations comprising the index. See *Index* in Section I. For a more detailed discussion on the major stock indexes refer to *Stock Indexes* in Section II.

STOCK INDEX FUTURE A futures contract on any of the stock indexes, including the NYSE index, S&P 500 or S&P 100, and The Value Line Index.

STOCK POWER An assignment allowing transfer of stock ownership from one party to another party. The stock power gives power of attorney to a third party, usually the transfer agent, to affect the stock ownership transfer between two other parties. See *Transfer Agent* in Section I.

STOP-LIMIT ORDER A buy or sell instruction to the securities broker to make the trade at the specified price or better but only after a specified stop price has been reached or passed. A stop-limit order to sell is effective as soon as there is a sale at the stop price or lower, and then it is executed, if possible, at the limit or higher. Such an order would read Sell 500 at 13 stop 12 limit. A stop-limit order avoids the risk associated with stop orders which become market orders when the stop price is attained but runs the risk of not completing the transaction at all if the limit price cannot be obtained. See *Stop Order* in Section I.

STOP LOSS An order instruction used by investors to protect existing profits or limit losses. The investor instructs the broker to set a sell price for the specific security at a price below the current market price. If the stock price drops to the stop loss price set by the investor, the order becomes a market order, thereby allowing the investor to close the position and preserve profits already earned or limit losses. See *Stop Loss* in Section II.

STOP ORDER An order instruction to a broker to buy or sell at the market prices as soon as the security has traded at a specific price known as the stop price. In a rising market, an investor may use stop orders to protect a gain. As the security's market price rises, the stop order is changed to protect the additional gain. If the stock should then drop to the stop price, the market order is executed, preserving the investor's gain.

STOPPED OUT When an investor's order is executed through a stop order at the specified stop price. For example, an investor has placed a stop price of $11 a share on XYZ, Inc. while its market price is $13 1/2. The market takes a tumble bringing XYZ, Inc. stock market price to $11 a share and the investor's sell order is executed. The investor has been said to have been stopped out.

STRADDLE Investment strategy combining put and call options on the same investment with the same exercise price and expiration date.

STREET NAME The holding of customers' securities by a brokerage firm in its name. The procedure allows for easier transfer of stock ownership and shares during sale transactions.

STRIKE PRICE Also called exercise price. The price at which an option or futures contract can be executed according to the terms of the contract. For example, a call option to purchase XYZ, Inc. at $12 a share through the September expiration date (XYZ, Inc. Sept 10) has a striking price of $12 a share. If XYZ, Inc. is currently trading at $14 1/2 a share and the investor believes that will probably be the top until the August expiration date of the call, he would execute the call option at $12 a share and earn $2 1/2 a share ($14 1/2-$12) less commissions.

STRONG FORM That part of the efficient market theory which states that prices reflect all information, public and private.

SUBORDINATED DEBENTURE A debenture bond with lower repayment rights than other senior contractual debt. Since the risk is higher, subordinated debentures tend to carry higher interest rates or have a higher discount in the secondary market.

SUBSCRIPTION PRICE The price at which existing shareholders can purchase additional shares in accordance with a rights offering or subscription right.

SUBSCRIPTION RIGHT A privilege granted by the corporation to existing shareholders allowing them to subscribe to shares of an upcoming issue before it is offered to the general investing public. The subscription ratio allows current shareholders to purchase new shares in proportion to the number of shares currently owned in relation to total outstanding shares. See *Right* and *Subscription Warrant* in Section I.

SUBSCRIPTION WARRANT A type of security that reflects the number of rights granted to a shareholder. The subscription warrant entitles the holder to buy a proportionate amount of shares at the subscription price. Subscription warrants have value in that they may be exercised or sold to others who want to subscribe to the new shares. Warrants are usually issued as sweeteners to enhance the marketability of debt or preferred stock issues. See *Subscription Right* and *Warrant* in Section I.

SUPPORT LEVEL The lower price level at which the stock price stops falling due to purchases by investors. As a stock reaches a support level, investors will purchase the shares in the hopes of participating in the anticipated price rise from the support level. Technical analysts chart stock prices to determine support levels and plan purchase timing. See *Resistance Level* in Section I. Also see *Tops and Bottoms* in Section II for a more detailed discussion and a support level chart.

SUSPENDED TRADING A halt in trading of a security, usually in advance of a major announcement, allowing the market to have an orderly assimilation of the news and prevent major order imbalances. At times, major news stories may break without advance warning and the specialist may have to suspend trading until the security's price is stabilized. Major news announcements that may require suspended trading include merger announcements, major mineral discoveries, indictments against corporate officers, and a substantial swing in earnings.

SWEETENER Special feature of a debt obligation or preferred stock added to promote marketability. Rights and warrants are two popular sweeteners. Others may include special convertible provisions. See *Kicker, Rights, Subscription Warrants* and *Warrants* in Section I.

SWITCH A commodity futures trading program that offsets a position in one delivery month and simultaneously opens a similar position in another delivery month for the same commodity.

SYSTEMATIC RISK The risk attributable to factors affecting all investments. Also called market risk or non-diversifiable risk.

T

10K, 10Q The annual and quarterly reports required by the SEC which must be filed by corporations traded on organized exchanges and the over-the-counter NASDAQ market. These reports contain a wealth of information for the investor. They are considered "must" reading for informed investors. Although annual reports contain the basics of financial reporting, the 10k features more in-depth information on the company's products, market segments, competitors, plant facilities, customers, management, and legal proceedings. The 10q quarterly reports issued since the last annual report will present more recent events affecting company earnings and operations. It provides more detailed information on quarterly results, earnings and expense classifications, and significant events than the quarterly earnings release or shareholders report.

TEAR SHEET Information sheet on individual companies published by Standard & Poor's. The name derives from the fact that brokers tear the sheets out of the ring binders and send them to their customers.

TECHNICAL ANALYSIS An investment technique which analyzes market and stock price and volume trends with the purpose of establishing buy and sell strategies. Technical analysts use charting and/or computer analysis programs to isolate price and volume movements which are believed to signal market and individual stock price movements. Most technical analysis is short- to intermediate-term, but followers of the Elliott Wave Theory look at long-term technical market movements. See *Charting* and *Fundamental Analysis* in Section I. Also refer to *Technical Analysis* in Section II for a more in-depth discussion.

TECHNICAL SIGN A price movement which technical analysis can identify as an important move or shift of direction in terms of its chart pattern.

TENDER To surrender shares in response to a tender offer by a corporation or others to purchase the shares at a specified price within a specific period of time.

TENDER OFFER A bid to buy any or all of a corporation's outstanding shares, usually at a premium to current market value, by an individual, group or corporation seeking control. The takeover tender offer must be filed with the SEC prior to public announcement.

TERM BOND A corporate or municipal bond with a single long-term maturity date.

THEORETICAL VALUE OF A WARRANT Formula value for a warrant which determines its intrinsic value. Since the theoretical value does not take into account market factors, the warrant will usually trade above the intrinsic value.

THIN MARKET A market characterized by a lack of liquidity. In such a market, there is little price continuity with prices varying considerably from one transaction to the next. A thin market is caused by a lack of buyers or sellers.

THIRD MARKET The over-the-counter dealers who create a market by specializing in buying and selling of listed securities.

TICK Price movement of a stock originally derived from ticker tapes. An uptick is an upward price movement, a downtick is a downward price movement.

TICKER SYMBOL The letters that are used to designate a particular stock for trading transactions. Trades are reported on the consolidated tape and on quote machines by the company's ticker symbol. For example, the ticker symbol for USX Corporation is X.

TIGHT MARKET A market for a specific security, or the market in general, that is characterized by very competitive, active trading. The spread between bid and ask prices is very narrow in tight markets.

TIME VALUE A factor used in determining the option premium for a particular option. It is also considered the difference between the premium of an option and its intrinsic value.

For instance, an option with a premium of $40 and an intrinsic value of $35 would have a time value of $5.

TOEHOLD PURCHASE The purchase of less than 5% of the outstanding stock of a company which is a target acquisition. After 5% has been acquired, notification to the SEC, the appropriate stock exchange, and the target company is made.

TOMBSTONE The newspaper advertisement placed by underwriters of a public distribution of securities. It is not an offer to sell or a solicitation of an offer to buy. It provides minimal information about the offer and refers readers to the prospectus for details of the issue. Many underwriters use tombstones to advertise their role in mergers, private placements, and acquisitions. See *Prospectus* and *Underwriter* in Section I.

TOP Stock or market high point which will be followed by a consolidation and/or decline in stock prices.

TOPS AND BOTTOMS Various chart patterns reflecting stock and market movements. See *Tops and Bottoms* in Section II for examples.

TOP-DOWN INVESTING Investment strategy concentrating on looking at the economic scenario first before narrowing down investment options in specific industries and companies. See *Bottom-up Investing* in Section I.

TOTAL RETURN The calculation of yield which takes into account both dividend and interest income plus appreciation of the investment principal. Total return for bonds is yield to maturity. For stocks, estimated return based on the security's price/earnings ratio is added to the dividend yield.

TOTAL VOLUME The total number of shares traded in a day whether on the stock exchanges or in the over-the-counter markets. For instance, a stock traded on the New York Exchange could also be traded on a regional exchange and in the over-the-counter market. The total volume for that stock would be the aggregate volume from all trades of the stock no matter where traded.

TRADING PATTERN The charted pattern of a stock or commodity which illustrates the long-term direction of its price action. The slope of the parallel lines connecting the highest prices and the lowest prices determines the overall price trend. See *Trendline* in Section I. Also refer to *Trading Pattern* in Section II for further details and an illustration of a trading pattern.

TRADING POST Designated locations on the exchange floor where specific securities are traded. Each of the 22 trading posts on The New York Stock Exchange handles about 100 stocks.

TRADING RING Specific area of the New York Stock Exchange where exchange-completed trades in listed bonds are executed.

TRADING RANGE The highest and lowest prices at which a security, or the market in general, has traded for a specific period. The *Wall Street Journal, Barron's, Investor's Business Daily,* and financial sections of major newspapers list the 52-week trading range of each stock. See *Range* in Section I.

TRADING UNIT The normal number of shares or bonds traded on the exchanges or over the counter. For stocks, 100 share units or round lots are the norm. See *Odd Lot* and *Round Lot* in Section I.

TRADING VARIATION The minimum incremental price variation allowable. For most trades, 1/8 of a point is the minimum price variation. However, some smaller stocks selling for several dollars or less will be traded in 16th or 32nds. Options with premiums below $3 per share may trade in 16ths. Bonds may be traded in 8th, 16ths, 32nds, or 64ths, depending on maturity.

TRANSFER AGENT The agent of the corporation appointed to maintain stock and bond records. Duties include registering and issuing certificates, transferring ownership and canceling certificates, and updating stock and bond ownership records on the company's books. Generally, commercial banks serve as transfer agents for corporations but some corporations perform their own transfer functions. See *Stock Power* in Section I.

TREASURIES Negotiable debt securities of the U.S. government. Treasury bills are short-term debt obligations that mature within one year of issue and are issued at a discount from face value. Treasury bills are issued in minimum denominations of $10,000 and in $5,000 increments.

Treasury bonds are long-term debt instrument with 10-year or longer maturity dates. Treasury bonds are issued in denominations of $1,000. Treasury notes are intermediate debt securities with 1-to-10-year maturity dates. Treasury notes are issued in denominations from $1,000 to over $1 million.

TREASURY STOCK Previously issued and outstanding stock which has been repurchased by the corporation and held in the company treasury. Treasury stock may be resold on the public market, used for company stock options and stock purchase plans for possible acquisitions of other companies. It is still considered issued but not outstanding.

TREND The long-term price movements in the market price of a security, commodity or the market in general. Trends over six months in length are considered primary trends while price movements running counter to the primary trend are termed secondary trends.

TRENDLINE A straight line connecting the top or bottom market prices on a technical analysis chart for a particular security or for the market in general. The trendline establishes the long-term price trend. The angle of the trendline indicates whether the price is in a rising or declining pattern. See *Trading Pattern* in Section I. Also refer to *Trendline* in Section II for more discussion and illustration.

TRIANGLE A stock or commodity stock pattern outlining a triangle within the charted price movements. The triangle has its base facing left and the apex facing right. Also called a pennant or wedge. See *Pennant* in Section I.

TRIPLE EXEMPTION Feature of some municipal bonds which are exempt from federal, state and local taxation. Generally, interest income from bonds issued in the state in which the bond owner as a resident has a triple exemption.

TURNAROUND A positive change in the fortunes of a company. Turnarounds can result from a number of factors including management change, new product lines or markets, new technology, major mineral finds, and refinancing. See *Turnaround* in Section II for detailed discussion of turnaround investment strategies.

TWO-DOLLAR BROKER Member of the New York Stock Exchange who executes orders on the floor of the exchange for other members having more volume than they can handle at a particular time. They also execute orders for firms who do not have their own exchange member on the floor. Originally called $2 brokers because their round lot commission was fixed at $2. Now commissions between $2 brokers and commission brokers are negotiated. Also called independent broker.

U

UNCOVERED OPTION Also called naked option. An uncovered option is any option that the buyer or seller does not have covered with an underlying security position. See *Cover, Covered Call, Naked Option* and *Underlying Security* in Section I.

UNDERLYING SECURITY In regard to stock options, the underlying security is the security which must be delivered when an option is exercised. Index options are settled in cash.

An underlying security is also the common stock that must be delivered by the corporation in exchange for subscription rights, subscription warrants, convertible bonds or convertible preferred stock. See *Subscription Right, Subscription Warrant,* and *Uncovered Option* in Section I.

UNDERMARGINED ACCOUNT A margin account failing to meet the minimum maintenance requirements of the New York Stock Exchange, NASD or individual brokerage firm, or the margin requirements of Regulation T of the Federal Reserve. It is possible to purchase securities for an account that is undermargined, but the broker must issue a margin call. See *House Maintenance Requirements, Maintenance Margin,* and *Margin Call* in Section I.

UNDERVALUED A stock with a market value that does not adequately reflect the true value of the firm. Stocks may be undervalued for various reasons including general market conditions, industry presently out of favor with investors, relatively small following of investors, future earnings potential not full recognized, and substantial difference between asset book value and market value.

UNDERWRITE A function performed by investment bankers whereby they purchase an issue of securities from the corporation for resale to the investing public. The underwriter assumes the risk from the time of purchase until resale of the issue to the public. The entire issue is purchased from the issuer at a discount for resale at a predetermined price. The underwriter stands to gain by the amount of the overall discount less the costs of selling the issue to the public.

Another common use of the term underwrite applies to best-efforts underwriting. This is when the investment banker acts as the issuer's agent in selling the issue but does not take a financial position and therefore no financial risk in the issue.

UNDERWRITER Anyone who purchases securities from an issuer for resale to the investing public. More generally, anyone who helps in the public sale of securities by an issuer.

UNDERWRITING SPREAD The difference between the public offering price and the price paid by the underwriter to the issuer. Also termed the discount.

UNIFORM PRACTICE CODE The National Association of Securities Dealers' (NASD) rules and procedures which govern the conduct and handling of over-the-counter transactions.

UNISSUED STOCK The amount of stock authorized but not issued. It does not include treasury stock which has been reclaimed by the corporation. Unissued stock may be sold, used in mergers and acquisitions, and issued as stock options. See *Treasury Stock* in Section I.

UNIT INVESTMENT TRUST An investment company that issues redeemable securities denominated in units which represent an undivided interest in a unit of underlying securities. Unit investment trusts are required to be registered with the SEC under the Investment Company Act of 1940. Unit investments trusts purchase a fixed portfolio of securities. Unit owners receive a proportional share of net income and, as the securities mature, a return of their investment principal.

UNLISTED SECURITY Any security not listed for trading on one of the exchanges. Unlisted securities are traded over the counter.

UNLISTED TRADING The practice of trading unlisted securities on an organized exchange. A specialist may apply with the SEC to request approval to make a market in an unlisted security. Approval may be granted in order to provide the benefits of an auction market to security trading.

UNWIND A TRADE The correction of a previously recorded trade made in error.

UNSYSTEMATIC RISK Risk attributable to facts unique to the security. Also termed non-market risk or diversifiable risk. See *Systematic Risk* in Section I.

UPSTAIRS MARKET Securities transaction not sent to the exchange floor for execution but completed by the broker in-house at a negotiated price. SEC rules govern such trades to ensure the client receives prices favorable to those available on the exchange floor. Upstairs market transactions may be negotiated with mutual funds handled by a specific brokerage firm.

UPTICK Security trade executed at a higher price than the preceding trade in the same security. SEC rules state that short sales can only be made on upticks or zero plus ticks. See *Last Sale, Minus Tick* and *Plus Tick* in Section I.

UPTREND Upward movement in the price of stock, commodity future or the market in general. See *Trading Pattern* and *Trendline* in Section I.

V

VALUE CHANGE The adjustment made to the stock price in accordance with the number of shares outstanding for the security. For instance, a two-for-one stock split of a stock that has a market price of $50 will result in a value change to $25 per share since the number of shares outstanding has doubled. The value change is made in order to equally weigh the group of stocks comprising an index.

VARIABLE ANNUITY A life insurance investment contract whose value is determined by the changing value of the underlying portfolio of debt and equity securities. Variable annuities may be purchased with a lump sum payment or a number of installment payments. The payout may be a stream of periodic payments which vary with the market value of the portfolio or a fixed payment amount with possible add-ons based on the increased market value of the underlying portfolio. See *Annuity* in Sections I and II and *Fixed Annuity* in Section I.

VARIABLE RATE SECURITY Any security with provisions for recalculating the rate of return based on specific indexes. The interest rate is recalculated at specific intervals based on changes in the underlying index or indexes.

VERTICAL LINE CHARTING Technical analysis chart technique that utilizes a vertical line to indicate the high and low for the period and a horizontal line to indicate the closing price. The chart over a period of time shows the trend of the security or market index being charted. See *Vertical Line Charting* in Section II for more discussion and an illustration of vertical line charting.

VERTICAL SPREAD An option trading strategy with the investor establishing both long and short option positions in the same underlying security with the same expiration dates but with different strike prices.

V FORMATION A stock or commodity chart pattern that outlines a "V". The trend is considered bullish if the "V" is upright and bearish if the "V" is inverted.

VOLATILE A stock, bond, commodity or market that is susceptible to rapid price variations. The measure of a stock's volatility to the market in general is called its beta. A beta greater than 1 indicates more volatility than others for a variety of reasons. The stock's industry may be very volatile. For instance, gold mining stocks and toy company stocks have histories of volatile price movements. See *Beta* and *Volatility* in Section I.

VOLATILITY The amount of price movement of a stock, bond, commodity or the market in general during a specific period. A measure of a particular security's volatility in relation to the market is termed its beta. See *Beta* and *Volatile* in Section I. Also, fluctuations in a security's or portfolio's return.

VOLUME The number of stock shares, bonds or commodity contracts traded during a specific period. Daily volumes are listed in major financial publications. Trading volume is followed for indications of market strength. For instance, sharp price rises on higher than normal volumes may signal a prolonged price rise in a security. Stock exchange trading volume is also closely watched for signals of the potential strength and direction of the market.

VOLUME DELETED The elimination of volume on the consolidated tape due to the tape being more than two minutes late in reporting security transactions.

W

WARRANT An option to purchase a stated number of common shares at a specified price within a specific period of time. Warrants are usually issued as sweeteners to enhance the marketability of debt or preferred stock issued. See *Common Stock Equivalent, Subscription Right* and *Subscription Warrant* in Section I. See also *Warrant* in Section II.

WASH SALE The purchase and sale of a security either simultaneously or within a short period of time. Wash sales used to manipulate stock prices are illegal. Wash sales occurring within 30 days can not qualify as tax losses under IRS rulings.

WEAK FORM The part of the efficient market theory that states that security prices reflect all price and volume data.

WASTING ASSET Security with a value for a limited time which will expire worthless sometime in the future. Options are wasting assets: if they are not exercised prior to the expiration date, they will become worthless.

WATCH LIST A compilation of securities under special surveillance to detect trading irregularities. Potential takeover moves, high volume trading surges, and wide price fluctuations may cause a firm's security to be placed on the watch list.

WATERED STOCK Dilution of share ownership by issuing additional shares to represent the same capitalization. Watered stock can also be created by excessive stock dividends, overvalued assets, and substantial operating losses.

WEDGE A stock or commodity chart pattern resembling a wedge. The wedge has its base facing left. Rising wedges generally are considered interruptions of a falling price pattern and falling wedges as interruptions of upward price movement. See *Triangle* in Section I. See *Wedge* in Section II for an illustration.

W FORMATION A stock or commodity chart pattern resembling the letter "W". The bottom portion of the "W" indicates the price has hit a support level twice and is resuming its price rise. See *Double Bottom* and *Double Top* in Section I.

WHEN DISTRIBUTED Security transactions conditioned on the secondary distribution of shares. Distributed shares come into play in the event of a proposed distribution of shares in a subsidiary.

WHEN ISSUED Security transactions conditioned upon the issuance of the shares. The settlement date is determined when the securities are available.

WHIPSAW Result of volatile price movements exposing investor to both upside and downside investment risk.

WHITE KNIGHT Company or individual coming to the rescue of a firm threatened by an unfriendly takeover. The white knight tenders a higher offer and arranges a friendly takeover. See *Greenmail* in Section I.

WHITE'S RATING Municipal bond ratings developed by White's Tax-Exempt Bond Rating Service. This classification system is based on the municipal trading markets instead of credit ratings on the bond issuer; it attempts to reflect appropriate yields for individual municipal bonds.

WINDOW DRESSING Security transactions that are initiated to present a better quarterly or yearly report to shareholders. Window dressing transactions have little long-term effect on the value of the mutual fund.

WITH OR WITHOUT With or without or "W.O.W." orders are limit orders which are executed either on the quotation or on the round-lot sale, whichever is effective. If the order is filled on the quotation, the odd-lot differential is subtracted from the bid in the case of a sale or added to the offer in case of a purchase. If the order is filled on the basis or a round lot sale, the rules for limit orders apply.

WORKING CAPITAL The excess of current assets over current liabilities. Working capital is composed of the firm's cash, marketable securities, accounts receivable, and inventory. See *Acid-test, Current Ratio* and *Quick Ratio* in Section I.

WORKING CONTROL The condition existing when a shareholder owning less than 51% of the shares or having less than 51% of the voting interest controls corporate policy and actions.

WRAPAROUND ANNUITY An insurance company contract that provides tax sheltered dividends, interest, and capital appreciation while allowing the subscriber some choice of fund investment.

WRITE OUT Transaction made by a specialist and within exchange guidelines involving the specialist's own securities inventory. A write out would entail a trade between the broker and the specialist followed by a separate trade with the client. Normal broker's commissions are charged for write out trades.

WRITER An investor that sells an option contract and earns premium income. The writer is obligated to deliver the security in the case of a call option or to purchase the security in the case of a put option. Options may be written covered (with the underlying security position) or naked (without the underlying security position). See *Covered Call* and *Naked Option* in Section I.

X

XD Abbreviation used to designate ex-dividend.

XR Abbreviation used to designate stocks trading ex-rights.

Y

YANKEE BOND An international bond issued by foreign banks and corporations but trading in U.S. dollars and registered for sale in the United States. Yankee bonds may have favorable tax status in certain countries.

YELLOW SHEETS Compilation of the National Quotations Bureau that lists bid and ask prices and firms that make a market in over-the-counter, traded corporate bond. See *National Quotation Bureau* and *Pink Sheet Stocks* in Section I.

YIELD An investor's percentage return on security investments. For stock, it is the return earned from common stock or preferred dividends. For bonds, it is the coupon rate of return divided by the bond purchase price. See *Current Yield* and *Total Return* in Section I.

YIELD ADVANTAGE The difference in the yield that can be earned investing in a convertible security versus the yield offered on the underlying common stock security. For example, if a convertible preferred security currently yields 8% and the common stock current yield is 4 1/2%, the yield advantage for the convertible preferred stock is 3 1/2%.

YIELD CURVE A graph illustrating the relationship of interest rate yields to time for various fixed-income securities of the same class. If short-term rates are lower, the yield curve is positive. If short-term rates are higher, the yield curve is negative. Usually, yield curves are positive since investors want to be compensated for the additional risk associated with investing for longer periods of time. Yield curves can help in the analysis of interest rate trends. See *Negative Yield Curve* in Section II.

YIELD EQUIVALENCE The interest rate which provides the same return for both tax-exempt and taxable securities.

YIELD SPREADS The relationships between bond yields and the particular features on various bonds such as quality, callability, and taxes. Also, the difference between stock dividend yield and the current yield on bonds. See *Current Yield* in Section I.

YIELD TO AVERAGE LIFE A yield determined by calculating interest return based on present cash flow and the average life of securities in the portfolio.

YIELD TO CALL The yield on a bond up to date of the first call as detailed in the bond indenture.

YIELD TO MATURITY The yield which will be earned if the bond is held to maturity. The calculation takes into account purchase price, maturity, redemption value, coupon yield, and interest payment dates. Cash flow reinvestment at the same market rate of interest is also assumed in determining yield to maturity.

Z

ZERO COUPON A security sold with no coupons and at a fraction of its face or maturity value. No interest is paid during the investment term but the zero coupon securities can be redeemed for full face value at maturity.

ZERO-MINUS TICK Executed transaction at the same round lot price as the previous trade of the same security but lower than the next previous price. For example, a trade at 15 with a previous trade of 15 and its previous trade of 16 is a zero-minus tick trade.

ZERO-PLUS TICK Executed transaction at the same round lot price as the previous trade but higher than the next previous trade. For example, a trade of 15 with a previous trade of 15 and its previous trade of 14 is a zero-plus tick trade.

SECTION II

This section of *Wall Street Words* provides a handy source of investment information, providing more in-depth data, charts and investment strategies than are normally found in single focus investment books or typical investment dictionaries.

Section II expands upon the easy-to-understand definitions listed in Section I. Charts, examples, and narratives illustrate how various investment strategies and tools can be put to use to help increase investment profits and prevent costly mistakes.

AMERICAN DEPOSITARY RECEIPTS (ADRs) ADRs make it easy to acquire stock in foreign companies.

Portfolio diversification represents one of the key principles of smart investing. While many investors take this to mean that they should diversify their investment holdings among stock in different companies, companies in different industries, and among different types of investment alternatives, they often disregard diversifying their investment portfolio geographically outside of the United States because they fear the vagaries of trading on foreign stock exchanges.

Fortunately, there is a way to purchase a stake in the fortunes of foreign companies without trading on foreign exchanges and without buying a pool of foreign companies via an international mutual fund. How can this be done? With an ingenious investment device termed an American Depositary Receipt or ADR for short.

Just what are ADRs? In effect, ADRs represent ownership interest in foreign securities deposited in a custodial account at a U.S. depositary institution. They are fully negotiable certificates and trade just like American securities on the New York Stock Exchange, American Stock Exchange, other exchanges, and in the over the counter market.

Overall, nearly 1,100 foreign securities trade as ADRs in the United states, representing companies with operations all over the globe, including Japan's well-known Fuji Photo Film and West Germany's Siemens to less-known companies such as Finland's Cultor and Papua New Guinea's Bougainville Copper. ADR issues represent a variety of industries from automobiles and consumer goods to chemicals and mining.

All ADRs are priced in U.S. dollars so you don't have to worry about keeping track of your investment in foreign currency. In fact, for all practical matters, you trade ADRs just like any other stock investment listed on the stock exchanges or traded over-the-counter. Generally, an ADR represents one share of stock.

ADRs present an opportunity for the U.S. investor to benefit from global diversification while avoiding the hassle of purchasing stock on foreign exchanges and dealing with foreign investment taxes, etc. Dividends on the underlying stock of the ADR are received by the depository bank who will send you a check in U.S. dollars for the dividend proceeds net of applicable foreign withholding taxes.

ADRs allow you to tailor your overseas investment objectives without having to submit to purchasing a basket of companies you may not want or having to learn the intricacies of trading in different foreign markets.

Another plus, you don't need to worry about trying to decipher annual reports and other corporate correspondence, since they're written in English. Also, the SEC requires listed ADRs to provide financial reporting comparable to that of American companies, thus making it easier to compare ADR performance with domestic investment alternatives.

ADRs can be either sponsored or unsponsored. The only difference is that foreign companies that sponsor ADRs must comply with all Securities and Exchange Commission (SEC) disclosure and reporting requirements. On the other hand, unsponsored ADRs are created by a bank and registered with the SEC to satisfy investor demand for a specific foreign security.

An unsponsored ADR status does not indicate a bad investment risk. Many leading international firms such as The Netherlands' Unilever sport unsponsored ADR securities.

Of course, there are some caveats. You may be charged small fees by the depository bank for handling cash dividends, which diminish your total return slightly. For unlisted ADRs, financial and other company information may be hard to come by, making it difficult to properly evaluate the firm and its continued place in your portfolio. Finally, the risk of foreign currency losses hangs over the company's financial results and your investment performance.

ADRs are not new on the investment scene. They trace their history back to 1927 when Guaranty Trust Company of New York, devised the unique security in order to make it easier to trade the bevy of British stocks that were popular with American investors at the time.

Investor interest in ADRs continues to surge. Over seven billion listed ADR shares traded in 1994—representing nearly $260 billion in trading volume, more than double 1992 levels.

A wealth of options exist for investors. There are ADRs available for companies located in more than 40 countries, from Australia to Zimbabwe. The United Kingdom leads with some 19 percent of available ADRs, followed by Australia with 16 percent. Other countries with major ADR representation include Japan, South Africa, Germany, Hong Kong, Italy, Mexico, France, The Netherlands, Singapore, Spain, and Sweden.

European companies, on the eve of a united economic Europe, are in a unique position to serve both the European and global markets. Recent events in Eastern Europe also open the doors to new market opportunities. Likewise, Pacific Rim countries continue to experience robust growth. But you must look beyond the particular region of the world you wish to invest in and ferret out those companies that will benefit from their region's economic growth and opportunities beyond their own borders.

ACCUMULATION AREA For years, money could be made by accumulating stock of Benguet Corporation, the Philippine gold mining and engineering concern, by purchasing the shares when they reached their low between $3 and $4 a share. The accompanying chart shows Benguet price fluctuations for the years 1982 to mid-1985. The ranges for 1982 and 1985 were 3 1/2–6 1/8 and 3 1/8–6 1/2 respectively.

Watch stock behavior to ferret out potential accumulation areas that can help add to your investment gains.

Chart 1
Benguet Corporation

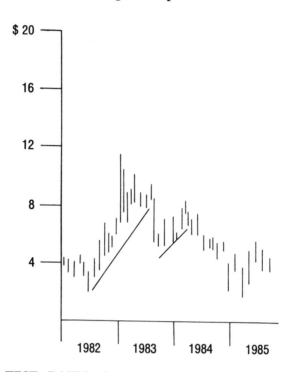

ACID-TEST RATIO Companies with equal current ratios (CA/CL) could have very different liquidity depending on the size of their inventory and its relation to total current assets. To illustrate, look at the following companies:

Chart 2

	Company A	Company B
Cash	$5 mil	$5 mil
Receivables	10	5
Inventory	5	10
Total Current Liabilities	$10 mil	$10 mil
Total Current Assets	$20 mil	$20 mil
Current Ratio	2 to 1	2 to 1
Acid-Rest Ratio	1.5 to 1	1 to 1

Although both companies have the same amount of cash and the same current ratios, Company A is a lot more liquid because less of its current assets are tied up in inventory:

$$\text{Acid--Test Ratio} = \frac{\text{Current Assets} - \text{Inventory}}{\text{Current Liabilities}}$$

ANNUITY An annuity allows earnings to appreciate tax-deferred until the annuity begins its payout period. If annuity payments are withdrawn prior to age 59 1/2, permanent disability, or death, a 10% penalty is invoked on top of the tax liability.

Fixed annuities guarantee a minimum rate of interest over the contract lifetime, usually with a higher rate for the first one to five years.

Variable annuities offer additional flexibility for the owner by allowing the movement of investments within a group of mutual funds.

Many annuities incur management fees, annual administrative charges, and either front-end load or back-end load costs associated with mutual fund investments. Make sure you understand all applicable charges and have your investment representative work through an example showing all fees and charges.

A well-placed annuity can provide investment security for retirement years with a minium of risk. Insurance companies are regulated and must retain minimum reserves, but there have been insurance companies who have filed for bankruptcy. A review of Best's Rating Service will give current rankings of insurance companies.

Hybrid annuities combine the best benefits of both fixed and variable annuities. The investor is allowed to invest a portion of the investment in a fixed annuity while the balance will be invested in a variable annuity.

Annuity payments can also be tailored to meet the investor's requirements. Immediate payment annuities are purchased with a lump sum payment and benefits begin immediately. On the other hand, deferred payment annuities postpone payments of benefits until a period of time has elapsed, perhaps until the annuitant reaches retirement age.

Annuities are attractive since they provide tax-free capital appreciation. Unlike IRA's, annuities are not limited to a yearly $2,000 contribution. Annuities can be purchased in units of $5,000 or more.

Of course, everything comes with a price. With annuities, it is the annual fees paid to the life insurance company. Fixed annuities typically carry a 2% fee for management and other expenses. Variable annuities can carry a front-end load of 3-4% on their mutual funds. Other plans carry a back-end load up to 9% for the first year and declining thereafter.

The annuity is basically a retirement vehicle. Uncle Sam frowns upon withdrawals before age 59 1/2, disability or death, imposing a 10% penalty on top of the tax liability.

Annuities offer a myriad of investment alternatives; take the time to find the right annuity for you. Pay attention to the financial stability of the insurance company offering the annuity you are considering. Make sure you receive a detailed record of all management, administrative, and surrender fees.

CALL OPTION A call option gives the holder the right to buy the specific stock at the exercise or "striking price" within a specified period of time.

Call options are purchased with the anticipation that the underlying stock will rise in value in excess of the premium paid for the call. When this happens, the holder can sell the call for a higher price, or can exercise the option and take delivery of the stock at a price less than current market value, either way enjoying highly leveraged gains.

The Chicago Board of Options and various brokerage houses provide option literature, usually free of charge. Easy-to-follow brochures explain the basics of options, illustrated with trading examples.

An important caveat: options are wasting assets, which means that their value expires if not exercised or sold before their expiration.

Options are traded on several exchanges such as the Chicago Board of Options, the American Exchange, and the Philadelphia Exchange. A review of the Listed Options Quotations page of the *Wall Street Journal* provides a current listing of stock in which options are traded. *Barron's* also provides a weekly summary of options trading as well as a narrative column on options. The following table was constructed from the Chicago Board of Options closing trades.

Chart 3

Option & NY Close	Strike Price	Calls—Last			Puts—Last		
		Sep	Oct	Dec	Sep	Oct	Dec
XYZ	10	1 5/16	r	2	r	3/16	r
11 3/8	12 1/2	1/16	5/16	3/4	1	1 3/8	1 7/8
11 3/8	15	r	1/16	3/8	r	3 3/4	r
11 3/8	17 1/2	r	r	3/16	r	6 1/4	r
11 3/8	20	r	1/16	1/16	r	r	r

r = not traded

The going price of an option is influenced by the price of the underlying security, the option striking price, underlying stock volatility, and remaining life of the option.

An option with a strike price that gives the right to buy a particular stock at less than its current market value is said to have intrinsic value or to be "in the money." In the chart, the XYZ call option with a strike price of 10 has intrinsic value because the stock's current market value is 11 3/8. The XYZ call options of 12 1/2, 15, 17 1/2 and 20 are currently "out of the money."

CASH FLOW ANALYSIS If King Midas were an investment analyst today, he might just forget about the Fed's interest rate moves, the global economy and balance of payment problems, quarter to quarter earnings projections, and the technical indicators and "elves" discussed on noted business investment programs. In Midas' day, cash was King.

Today, it's time to take a serious look at cash flow and cash positions of investment alternatives. No matter how good a piece of real estate may be in terms of potential value, if the income stream does not meet payment obligations, the property, in all likelihood, will have to be sold. Likewise, if a company has insufficient cash flow and reserves to capitalize on strategic opportunities, it may well lose out to competitors.

Cash flow is often a far better barometer of a company's financial health than earnings. A healthy cash position and attractive cash flow provide the company with the financial resources to raise outside capital, make strategic acquisitions, construct new plant facilities, carry on research and development, meet bond interest and other business obligations, pay dividends, and have the financial depth to weather economic recessions. Cash flow is the pulse of the company.

It should also be no surprise that cash-flow analysis can be an invaluable tool for the investor. In fact, more traditional accounting procedures often provide a distorted picture of a company's true financial health, so many professional investment managers and business consulting firms have long used cash-flow analysis as a key determinant in estimating the economic value of an investment.

The emerging realization of the importance of cash flow is highlighted by the Federal Accounting Standards Board (FASB) Statement No 95, Statement of Cash Flows. In short, the new FASB rule requires public companies to issue annual cash flow statements in addition to the usual financial reports. The move benefits investors wanting to judge the company on the strength of cash flow and changes in cash positions.

FASB Statement No. 95 is effective for annual financial statements for fiscal years after July 15, 1988. It requires that information about investing and financing activities not resulting in cash receipts or payment be provided separately so investors can take the information into account during their analysis. The implementation of this rule yields more uniform presentation of cash flow information, making comparison between alternative investments a lot easier.

Obviously, cash-flow analysis can help the investor zero in on investment opportunities that are not apparent when just tracking a company's earnings pattern. In addition, using cash-flow guidelines may help position the investor in a company before takeover offers run up its stock price.

To help in the search for companies with comfortable cash positions, impressive cash-flow streams, and/or improving cash scenarios, study the following terminology of cash-flow analysis.

Definitions

Cash-Flow/Debt Ratio The relationship of free cash flow to total long-term indebtedness. This ratio is useful in tracking a firm's ability to meet scheduled debt and interest payment requirements.

Cash-Flow/Interest Ratio This ratio determines how many times free cash flow will cover fixed interest payments on long-term debt.

Common and Preferred Cash-Flow Coverage Ratios These determine how many times annual free cash flow will cover common and preferred cash dividend payments.

Economic Value The economic value of a stock is the anticipated free cash flow the company will generate over a period of time discounted by the weighted cost of a company's capital.

Free Cash Flow Free cash flow can be determined by calculating operating earnings after taxes and then adding depreciation and other noncash expenses, less capital expenditures and increases in working capital.

Free-Cash Flow/Earnings Ratio The percentage of earnings actually available in cash. It is the amount of free cash available to company management for investments, acquisitions, plant construction, dividends, etc. As a general rule, this ratio should be, at a minimum, 0.5:1. In other words, at least 50 percent of the earnings should be in the form of free cash.

CLOSED-END FUND A closed-end fund is an investment fund that issues a fixed number of shares at its inception. These shares trade on a securities exchange as a stock would.

There are plenty of opportunities for investors in closed-end funds, but there are also risks. For starters, an investor must avoid investing in a new-issue, closed-end fund selling at a high premium. Choose a fund with superior compound-growth track records that fully discloses information to the investor.

Since a new-issue, closed-end fund has no track record, its premium is tied more to stiff underwriting expenses than to the fund's potential earnings capability. Underwriting spreads on closed-end funds can be as high as eight percent. Typically, new-issue closed-end funds tend to fall in price during the months after initially being sold to the investing public.

Stay away from new closed-end fund issues until the underwriting premium has been absorbed and the fund trades on its own merits. Follow the fund for at least six months and track the fund's performance in relation to investment objectives detailed in the prospectus.

Probably the biggest advantage of closed-end funds is management's ability to fully utilize investment funds, since they do not have to maintain large cash reserves for share redemption. In addition, lower expense ratios than open-end funds mean more cash is kept in the fund, generating returns for shareholders.

Closed-end funds can be used to tap specialized investment objectives. For instance, there are closed funds covering market niches such as municipal bonds, convertible securities, industry sectors, and overseas equities. As in any investment alternative, look at the market liquidity and particular investment focus in light of both domestic and international economic scenarios.

The closed-end fund investor can choose from a wide variety of investment options. There are funds specializing in traditional bonds while other funds target the convertible bond market. Other specialities include municipal bonds, overseas equities and industry securities. Of course, a number of diversified closed-end funds are also available.

While mutual funds trade at their net asset value (N.A.V.) and managers must frequently redeem and issue shares, closed-end funds have a limited, fixed number of shares that trade like stock on exchanges. Therefore, their trading price at any given moment is determined both by the funds' N.A.V. and investor sentiment toward the particular fund and its future earnings prospects. In fact, it is rare that a closed-end fund actually trades at its N.A.V.

After the initial offering, closed-end funds have traditionally traded at a discount to their N.A.V. For instance, if a fund with a million shares outstanding has holdings worth $10 million, you would expect a trading range of 9 3/4 to 10 1/4. But more often than not, the fund will trade around 9. In other words, you receive $10 of assets for every $9 invested, a 10 percent discount. A discounted fund offers a degree of safety. As the N.A.V. declines, generally the share price will decline less proportionally.

To illustrate, during a market decline the N.A.V. may fall 20 percent from $10 to $8 while the fund's share price discount may actually narrow. In this case, the share price might drop to $7.20 from $8.00 a share, only a 10 percent decline. Of course, such movement is not guaranteed and a decline in the N.A.V. may be compounded by a widening of the discount, dealing closed-end fund investors accelerating losses. Most experts agree that purchasing closed-end funds at a discount is the prudent way to capitalize on this unique investment alternative.

Some people suggest that investors buy a closed-end fund whenever its discount from N.A.V. reaches 20 percent. But more cautious investors shun the mechanical approach. They realize that there can be important reasons for a wide discount from asset value. For example, the fund's underlying investments may be underperforming the general market. Instead, experts suggest that you consider buying a closed-end fund when its discount from N.A.V. reaches or exceeds its own historical discount.

There's another twist to closed-end fund investment. In recent months, several funds have "open-ended" or converted to open-end mutual fund status allowing investors to sell out their shares at their full per share portfolio value, less a redemption fee. If you were lucky enough to buy a closed-end fund selling at a 20 percent discount and it later open-ended, you would earn an immediate 20 percent gain.

COVERED CALLS Covered calls offer the investor a unique opportunity to profit further on current stock holdings. A covered call is a call option written on securities owned by the option writer. Call options can be written against stocks, warrants, convertible bonds, convertible preferreds, and other calls.

Some advantages of writing covered calls—

1. The premium received from writing the call is insurance against a possible drop in the stock price.

2. The premium increases the yield on the security invest-ment over the basic dividend or interest yield. A 20 percent yield on covered call options is a respectable yield increase.

3. The security can effectively be purchased at a discount from the current market price by writing a covered call while simultaneously buying the security.

4. The opportunity exists to participate in stock price appre-ciation (restricted by the option striking price) while earn-ing a premium from the call sale.

5. The relatively short life of the covered call limits the risk of losing the underlying security, especially in a market trad-ing in a narrow range.

6. Covered calls can be sold again and again after each expi-ration, thereby increasing yield.

There are also several drawbacks to writing covered calls. First, you have to hold the security until the option expires and run the risk that the stock may decline more in value than you earn from the call premium. Second, you forfeit the opportunity to participate in the security's advance beyond the striking price.

EXAMPLES: Referring again to the chart of XYZ options (Chart 3), several option writing strategies are available. Covered calls can be written for varying expiration periods (September, October, December). Options expire on the Saturday following the third Friday of the expiration month. The following exam-ples ignore commissions to keep calculations simple.

Example 1: Assume you own 500 shares of XYZ which you purchased at $7 per share.

You write a December call with a strike price of 10 and receive $1,000 ($2 x 500) which protects the gain from 7 to 11 3/8 that you have already earned. If the stock declines, the $1,000 will help offset the price decline.

Example 2: You can effect a discount in the price of the stock by simultaneously writing a call option. If you purchase 500 shares at the current price of 11 3/8 and also write a De-cember call with a strike price of 12 1/2 for a premium of 3/4 you will receive $375 thereby resulting in a net cost of $5,312 ($5,687-$375). The savings is nearly 6.6 percent.

Example 3: XYZ's indicated dividend rate is $1.20 a year, resulting in a yield of 10.5 percent based on a purchase price of $11 3/8. By writing covered calls on a regular basis, the stockholder can reasonably expect to raise his yield considerably. Assume you write covered calls twice a year and average 1/2 in premium. Your yield would rise to 19.3 percent a year.

Sophisticated and neophyte investors alike can benefit from option trading. If you believe the stock will trade in a narrow range, want to increase the yield on your investment, or want to protect your stock position and gains, then writing calls may be for you

For a glossary of option terms, refer to *Option* in Section II.

CONVERTIBLE Many investors are missing unique opportunities because they do not understand convertible terminology and the basics of convertible investing. Convertible securities are hybrid investments because they possess attributes of both stocks and bonds. Convertible preferred stocks and convertible bonds are very similar so the following discussion of convertible bonds generally applies to convertible preferred stocks as well.

Since the convertible can be exchanged for the common stock, the market value of the convertible usually rises and falls in conjunction with the common stock. Prices of convertibles normally rise slower than the common stock until the stock rises materially above the conversion price (the conversion price is the common stock price at which the convertible holder breaks even on the conversion). Then the convertible's upside potential correlates closely with common stock price movements. Conversely, as the price of the common stock falls, the convertible price declines at a slower rate due to its interest-paying capability, allowing it to trade like a true bond. In this way, the investor gets the best benefit of both bond and common stock ownership.

A convertible bond is a fixed income security since its interest yield will remain constant after purchase. An attractive yield can be locked in while waiting for the underlying stock to increase in value. The hybrid attributes enable the investor to earn a yield higher than that obtainable from the underlying common stock dividends while sharing in the stock's price appreciation. At the same time, the investor is protected in a declining market by the interest earnings paid by the convertible bond.

Besides offering both interest and price appreciation opportunities, convertibles also occupy a senior position to common stock in the capital structure of the company. Holders of convertibles always receive their interest or dividend payments prior to holders of common stock. In addition, they also have a superior claim on company assets over common stock holders in the event of liquidation or bankruptcy.

The convertible market is normally strongest during a bull market for stocks and increasing yields from declining interest rates. Technically, stock market booms followed by consolidation periods present reasonable buys in the convertible market. If the surge resumes, convertible investors are sure to share in the gains. If stocks move sideways or decline, the bond features take over and regular interest payments add to earnings.

Companies are attracted to convertibles because they carry a lower coupon or dividend rate than straight bonds or preferred stock. They also normally sell at a premium due to the convertibility provision.

Firms offering convertibles run the gamut from the bluest of blue chips to struggling new firms. It pays to check the value and track record of the issuing company. *The Wall Street Journal, Barron's, Investor's Business Daily* and the major daily newspapers carry convertible bond listings. Look for the symbol "cv" to determine which issues are convertible.

Blue chip issues have attracted large financial and corporate funds to the convertible market, thereby providing greater liquidity for convertible trading. A number of mutual funds now specialize in convertible trading ranging from conservative to high yield junk bond strategies. If mutual funds are your investment vehicle, take your time to analyze the available investment information and choose wisely as you would for any investment.

A note of caution is in order. Convertible bonds frequently carry a redemption clause that permits the issuing company to redeem or call the securities before maturity. If called, the holder must redeem the securities for cash. If the bonds are trading higher than the call price, the investor could stand to lose the difference between the convertible's market price and the call price. Convertible calls tend to happen near market peaks when convertible issues are trading higher than the call price due to substantial price increases in the underlying common stock. Savvy companies can call the convertibles, leaving investors holding the bag. Check out the call provisions-both the call price and the earliest call date. Avoid issues without favorable clauses.

CONVERTIBLE STRATEGIES Two particularly attractive convertible bond trading strategies involve the corporate turnaround candidate and the company that is not actively or widely followed by the market.

Convertible issues of turnaround candidates are especially attractive since interest earnings can accumulate—usually at very attractive yields—during the months and years that it takes management to engineer a successful turnaround. The turnaround convertible can generally be picked up at a deep discount since the company's fortunes have waned and its stock and bond issues have fallen out of favor with investors. The general market views the bond as a busted convertible with little chance that the stock will rise sufficiently in value to trigger the conversion feature. In addition, the bond's yield is high compared to other bonds paying the same interest rate but not discounted in price.

Unfortunately, not all turnaround attempts come to a triumphant conclusion. Some detective work is needed to ferret out the special situations that merit investment. Certain factors should be considered in selecting a turnaround convertible: the fundamental financial strength of the company; economic and competitive conditions affecting the company and its industry; and the company's short-and long-term growth prospects based on anticipated economic forecasts.

Prime candidates for potential turnaround convertibles can be located in depressed cyclical industries that are bottoming out. Smaller industrial companies generally react quicker and capitalize on improving economic conditions. Be on the lookout for evidence that the company is working hard on improving its fortunes. Clues that are readily available in *The Wall Street Journal* and *Barron's* include reports of top management changes and restructuring of company operations through acquisitions, plant shutdowns, and sale or spin-off of unprofitable divisions.

Other situations that contribute to turnaround opportunities are new and unique product lines or services, technological breakthroughs, mergers, or takeovers. In the case of natural resource companies, there may be a significant mineral or oil/gas discovery.

To illustrate: A look at the dramatic Republic Airlines turnaround (that culminated in Republic's purchase by Northwest Airlines) is warranted. Republic was being battered by fare wars, rising fuel costs, and high labor costs. By 1983, Republic posted four straight years of losses totaling over $220 million. Its stock had dropped like a rock from a five-year high of $11.82 to $3 a share, while its 10 1/8% 2007 convertible bonds languished in the mid-$60 range.

The first hint of Republic's resurgence came with the announced hiring of Stephen Wolf as executive vice president and chief operating officer and it didn't take Wolf long to rise to president and chief operating officer and embark on a raid of major airlines for needed executive talent. Improved financial controls, including tight cost containment and zero-based budgeting, helped get costs back in line. Upgrading the fleet and tighter purchasing controls shaved pennies per gallon of fuel, resulting in millions of dollars in cost savings. Labor negotiations generated $100 million in savings annually in exchange for profit-sharing stock packages for company employees. All in all, management actions halted mounting losses and helped Republic post a $29.5 million gain in 1984, compared to a $111 million loss in 1983.

A Republic 10 1/8% 2007 convertible bond purchased in mid-February 1984 at 67 3/4 would have locked in a yield of over 15% while waiting for the turnaround to unfold. Republic's convertible bonds nearly doubled by December 1985, prior to the announced merger with Northwest Airlines and a calling-in of bonds. Investors in the Republic convertibles had their cake—and ate it too. Decide on an investment strategy that fits your temperament. Whether you are ultra-conservative or a speculator, there is probably a convertible for you.

Another tactic involves finding market anomalies in convertibles that do not have a large market following. Spend time evaluating convertible bond trading patterns for thinly followed issues.

A number of timely buy orders placed several points below, and sell orders placed several points above the market during that period could be executed at very favorable prices and profits.

No matter which convertible bond strategy you choose, it is imperative that you learn as much about the company as you can. Call the investor relations department and ask for the company's annual report and 10k. Also spend time in the business section of your library. Many have copies of *Value Line Convertibles* for your use.

A review of terms unique to convertibles is a key to understating convertibles.

The conversion rate or ratio is the rate at which a $1,000 par value bond may be converted into shares of common stock. The conversion price is the amount of par value exchangeable for one share of common stock. To determine the number of shares allowable in a conversion, divide the $1,000 par value by the conversion price. For example, a bond with a conversion price of $20 will convert into 50 shares of common stock (1,000/20).

Conversion equivalent is the adjusted price at which stock must sell to be of equal value with the bond. The following formula shows how the conversion equivalent is calculated:

$$\text{Conversion Equivalent} = \frac{\text{Market Price of Bond}}{\text{Number of Shares Received}}$$

A bond selling at 104 and convertible into 30 shares of underlying stock has a conversion value of $34.67 (1040/30). Assume that the stock is selling for $40 a share. The investor could convert and earn a profit before commissions of $5.33 per share ($40.00-$34.67). If the stock price is $34.67 or below, there is no advantage in converting so the investor would continue to hold the bond and earn the fixed interest.

In reality there is usually no need to go through the conversion process because the market value of the convertible security will rise to reflect the increased value for the underlying common stock. But remember, the market is not perfect and anomalies do exist.

The convertible premium is the portion of the bond selling price in excess of its conversion value. The parity is the value of the bond without the premium. The price of the common, the convertible, and parity value constantly fluctuate. The length of time it takes to repay, in interest, the amount paid over its conversion value is called the premium payback period. For example, if a bond purchased at $250 premium pays $125 annual interest, then it will take two years to break even.

DIVIDEND REINVESTMENT Many investors miss out on investment compounding opportunities by being unaware of the benefits offered by dividend reinvestment plans or DRIPs as they are called in the industry.

To the individual investor, DRIPs offer a number of advantages. First of all, the broker's commission bite, which can be substantial for small lot purchases, is bypassed. Companies absorb the cost of purchasing and issuing shares to plan members. In fact, many companies allow the sale of company stock through the program, thereby allowing you to avoid commissions on both ends of the investment trade.

Another plus for investors who want to accumulate shares in excess of that available from dividend reinvestment is that most plans allow additional purchases of shares within minimum and maximum dollar ranges at specific investment dates. Check the plan description for details.

A few companies offer their stock at a discount to market price to entice dividend reinvestment participation and thus locking in an immediate gain for the investor. Tax law changes have resulted in some firms dropping the discount feature, but some sleuthing could uncover companies that still offer this unique benefit.

The ease of adding to your stock holdings is another selling point for dividend reinvestment plans. Once the initial paperwork is out of the way, your stock portfolio grows without any intervention on your part.

By far the best attribute of DRIPs is the compounding effect of reinvesting your dividends. For example, a stock yielding 10 percent annually would return your original investment in ten years; however, if you reinvested the dividend and allowed it to compound at the same rate, it would only take seven years and three months to payback your original investment.

DRIPs fall into four types: full reinvestment, partial reinvestment, cash purchase only, and a combination thereof. Some plans require certain percentages or number of shares to participate, and others limit the cash-payment option to shareholders who participate in the dividend reinvestment plan.

While 81 percent of the plans absorb all costs of purchasing additional stock through reinvested dividends, the trend is toward the shareholder absorbing more of the costs of DRIP transactions. For example, in 1989, AT&T (NYSE:ATT) instituted a service charge of $1 or 10 percent of the dividend, whichever is smaller.

Through the cash-purchase plans, offered by more than 87 percent of the plans in 1994, shareholders can purchase additional shares of stock ranging from $25 a month up to $5,000 a quarter.

Other wrinkles unique to specific DRIPs include a discount on the price paid for the shares. For example, Bay State Gas (NYSE:BGC), Mellon Bank (NYSE:MEL), and First Union Corp. (NYSE:FTU) offer a 3 percent discount from market price.

Gerber Products (NYSE:GEB) and Motorola Inc. (NYSE:MOT) permit shareholders to use the dividends from one shareholder account to purchase shares for another account. To illustrate, your Gerber common-stock cash dividends could be used to purchase shares in your child's or grandchild's account. In some plans, dividends from preferred shares may be invested in the common stock of the same company.

You won't escape the tax bite by reinvesting your dividends. The reinvested dividend is taxable to the plan participant, and so is the difference between the fair-market-value price and any discounted price you receive.

There are some minor drawbacks which should be noted. Obviously if you need dividend income to meet living expenses, reinvestment plans are not for you. Also, current tax law considers reinvested dividends taxable even though you do not receive the cash.

Despite the paperwork involved in handling DRIPs, companies also like the plans. The lower cash payout conserves capital within the companies helping to reduce costly outside financing requirements. Shareholders participating in DRIPs are generally long-term investors in the company stock resulting in less overall administrative paperwork associated with a changing shareholder base. Another boon to companies sponsoring DRIPs—long-term shareholders tend to purchase the company's goods and services in the marketplace.

Overall, the benefits far outweigh the drawbacks and dividend reinvestment plans make sense for the majority of investors. Instead of cashing your dividend checks and frivolously spending money, put those funds back to work compounding your investment return. Dividend reinvestment information is usually provided in the inner back page of company annual reports. Basic terms are briefly listed along with an address for requesting additional information and the plan prospectus. Read the plan agreement carefully to make sure you understand all its covenants.

Your broker can also help find out if a particular company offers a reinvestment plan. *Value Line* and *Standard & Poor's* tear sheets list whether reinvestment plans are available. Both can be found in most city and university libraries.

Evergreen Enterprises P.O. Box 763, Laurel, MD 20725-0763 publishes a handy guide titled "Directory of Companies Offering Dividend Reinvestment Plans." It's a good idea to call the company directly to verify plan terms before purchasing the stock, since many changes occur to programs each year.

The National Association of Investors Corporation (NAIC) in Madison Heights, MI, features a "Low-Cost Investment Plan" specifically designed to take advantage of DRIPs. It allows beginning investors to accumulate a stock portfolio without having their investment stake eaten up by high commissions.

The NAIC program offers two main benefits: you don't have to purchase shares of a company on your own in order to join their DRIP, since the NAIC already owns shares in a number of DRIPs; further, it saves time and eliminates the need for you to request and fill out your own DRIP application forms.

Joining a DRIP is simple. After purchasing at least one share of company stock, just fill in the application form (usually obtained by calling the investor relations department of the company) and mail it to the company or bank administering the plan. Typically, your account becomes effective with the next dividend payable if your authorization is received before the dividend record date.

Literally hundreds of firms traded on the New York and American exchanges and over-the-counter have DRIPs.

Dividend reinvestment plans offer investors a chance to improve their return. Investigate available plans and choose one that fits your needs.

FINANCIAL REPORT READING Settle into a comfortable chair with a good underlining or highlighting pen. Read the information through once to get a feel for the company, its products and services, general financial condition, and operational scope. Highlight points you want to remember; jot down key words in a margin as a quick reference.

Now turn to the management discussion and analysis of operations. The company is required by the SEC to present an accurate portrayal of events that materially affected operations during the past fiscal year. Look for discussion of products, pricing, inventory writedowns, acquisitions and divestitures, and sales and earnings trends.

Pay particular attention to extraordinary items such as increased earnings due to pension plan accounting adjustments or gains or losses on sales of surplus equipment. Remember to isolate earnings from continuing operations and the extraordinary one-time events. After all, you will be investing in the continuing operations of the company. Continue to ask yourself two questions: why did this happen and what does it mean for the future? The letter to the shareholders tends to contain more upbeat information. Use it to learn more about events or circumstances which will positively affect future earnings. For instance, a new mineral discovery bodes well for a mining firm several years in the future. The time to start accumulating a position is before the increased earnings stream comes on line.

Check to make sure the company's annual report is not "qualified" by its public accountants. That generally means trouble and the company could be on the verge of some very serious financial, operating and/or legal difficulties. Otherwise, the auditor's opinion states the company's annual report conforms to "generally accepted accounting principles applied on a basis consistent with the prior year."

Keep the 10k handy. It contains more in-depth information on the company's products, market segments, competitors, plant facilities, customers, management, and legal proceedings.

Is the company a major force in the marketplace or at the mercy of the industry giants? Is the company heavily dependent on one or several customers for a major portion of its sales? Does it have a steady source of raw materials or is it heavily dependent on oil feedstocks where availability and price can fluctuate rapidly and widely? Where are its manufacturing plants located, how are union relations, is the company updating facilities with capital appropriations? All of these questions need to be asked and answered in your review of company information.

Check the schedules of repair and maintenance and advertising expenses in the 10k. Make sure the increased earnings are not the result of postponed expenses which will catch up to the company in the future.

Management experience and their past record of proven results is a key to the company's future. Pay attention to management changes and years of industry and/or marketing experience of company officers as listed in the 10k. Too often existing management is tied to past decisions to effect a turnaround. Top management changes often signal a potential turnaround candidate. For example, Stephen Wolf's hiring for the top slot at Republic Airlines set the stage for the tough decisions that needed to be made and Republic's dramatic turnaround. Republic is now part of Northwest Airlines.

The quarterly report issued since the last annual report will present more recent events affecting company earnings, operations, and its future. Again, the 10q (quarterly equivalent of the annual 10k) will provide more detailed information on quarterly results, earnings and expense classifications, and significant events.

After a thorough understanding of the company and its operation has been obtained, it is time to turn to the footnotes, long-term debt, working capital, and liquidity and ratio analysis.

Despite being relegated to the rear of the annual report, in print smaller than the bulk of the annual report, footnotes contain a wealth of information. The investor must take care to read footnotes thoroughly and interpret their impact on past, current, and future operating results.

Ferret out any changes in accounting procedures that have a significant effect on the comparison of successive years' financial statements. For example, a change in the method of calculating inventory could boost operating profit while raising inventory value. FIFO (first in, first out) inventory valuation will result in a lower cost of goods sold and a higher profit when prices are rising. Future earnings could be impaired as the low cost inventory is worked off.

Many companies have revised their pension plan actuarial assumptions taking advantage of higher rates of return earned in recent years. This will result in large extraordinary gains in current year results.

Other accounting changes for which one needs to watch: a change in the allowance for bad debts, a change in the depreciation life of plants and equipment, and the reclassification of current receivable to long-term receivables.

Acquisition and divestiture information will be both footnoted and detailed in the 10k report. Does the company have a proven track record of successful acquisitions or is the present acquisition a new and potential dangerous change in operations.

Taxes can be a contributing factor in earnings swings. Special tax credits and tax-loss carryforwards can help to shelter future earnings from taxes and deliver greater returns to company stockholders in increased equity or higher dividends.

Company intentions to repurchase stock will be reported in a footnote. By retiring stock, the company can increase earnings and dividends per share. Stock splits and stock dividends also will be reported in footnotes.

The firm's long-term debt structure lists obligations, rates, and maturities. Compare rates on company debt with current financing rates to see if the company has to pay a premium for financing. Look for innovative low-cost financing arrangements such as industrial revenue bonds or overseas financing.

How much of long-term debt is convertible with potential dilution of stockholder's equity and earnings per share? Are maturities scheduled out over a long period or are there major refinancings or payoffs scheduled in the near future?

Hand in hand with long-term debt, short-term credit needs to be evaluated. The company should have adequate untapped short-term credit arrangements for current operating requirements, planned capital expenditures, and potential emergency situations. Many companies keep a "shelf" registration of securities as well as banking credit lines.

The company's working capital reveals the size of funds readily available, but its current ratio shows how many times current liabilities are covered by current assets. In general, the higher the current ratio, the more short-term financial strength. However, too high of a current ratio may indicate company resources not being put to efficient use. A declining ratio may be indicative of trouble or it may be cyclical contraction.

The debt-to-equity ratio indicates the amount of leverage a company uses to generate earnings. By using leverage effectively, management can increase earnings per share returns for stockholders. But too much debt carries high interest payments and large obligations which may become too burdensome for the company in a declining market or economy.

Book value per share does not represent the firm's true value in liquidation, obsolete plants may not command book value while land holdings may have a far greater market value than carried on the company's balance sheet.

Inconsistencies in asset value also distorts shareholders' equity. For example, marketable securities must be carried at the lower of cost or market value. If the securities have risen substantially in value, current assets, book value, and stockholders' equity will all be understated.

Operating statistics also provide insight to company fortunes. What does the sales trend look like? Are operating costs, as a percentage of sales, rising or declining? Have earnings per share been on a consistent growth pattern or erratic? Are dividends increasing, and what is the dividend payout ratio? If you plan to hold the stock for a long time, what is the stock's yield in relation to other investment alternatives? How does its price/earnings ratio (PE) compare to the market in general and other companies in the same industry?

Spend time to become an informed investor; your investment in time will pay dividends.

FUNDAMENTAL ANALYSIS Being an informed investor means learning as much about the company as you can.

Fundamental analysis uses financial and other information to help you become an informed investor.

The most obvious source of corporate financial information is the company itself. Most companies are very receptive to inquiries from stockholders and potential stockholders. A short letter requesting information will be responded to in a reasonable amount of time. If you desire information on a more timely basis, a quick phone call to the Investor or Public Relations office is in order. Just tell the receptionist you wish to receive some annual reports and you will be directed to the right people. Don't let the price of a phone call prevent you from requesting information. That $1.50 call can save you hundreds or thousands of dollars by avoiding a bad investment decision.

Press releases will keep you up to date on new products, management changes, and acquisitions. The proxy statement provides a detailed background of company management and directors. If the company has completed or is in the process of a public offering of stock or bonds, ask for the prospectus. It discusses the company's operations, finances and management.

GAP The pattern in a chart when the price for one day's trading does not overlap the previous day's price range. The chart illustrates a gap between the closing price of 25 1/2 on one day and the opening price of 26 on the following day.

Chart 4

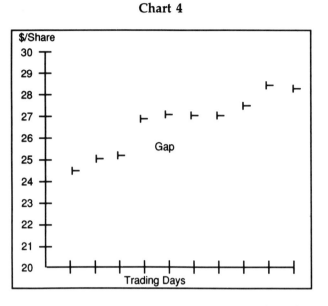

HEAD AND SHOULDERS A stock or commodity chart pattern outlining the head and shoulders of a person.

The chart illustrates the top of the head around 27 1/2
and the shoulders peaking around 26.

Chart 5

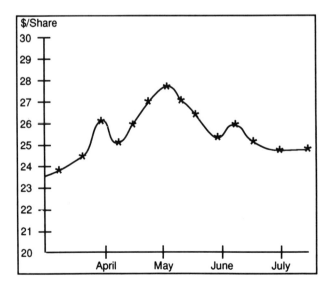

HORIZONTAL PRICE MOVEMENT The chart pattern of a security trading in a narrow price range.

In the chart, the security is trading in a top around 23 1/2 and a bottom around 22 3/4.

Chart 6

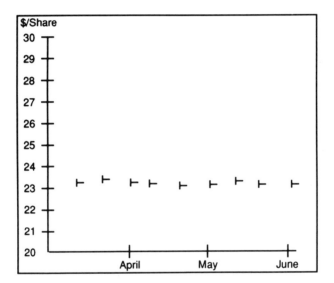

INDICATOR Indicators are measurements of the U.S. economy or securities market that help economists and investment analysts to understand, interpret, and predict economic and financial events.

The U.S. Department of Commerce publishes the index of leading indicators (adjusted for inflation) as a tool for forecasting cyclical advances and declines in the country's business cycle.

The most recent components of the Index of Leading Indicators are authorized housing permits, average production workweek, average weekly unemployment insurance claims, business investment (net), business and consumer borrowing, change in inventory, consumer goods new orders, plant and equipment orders, sensitive material prices, stock prices, vendor performance, and M2-money supply.

In addition to the official list of economic leading indicators, many investors find value in some stock market leading

Chart 7

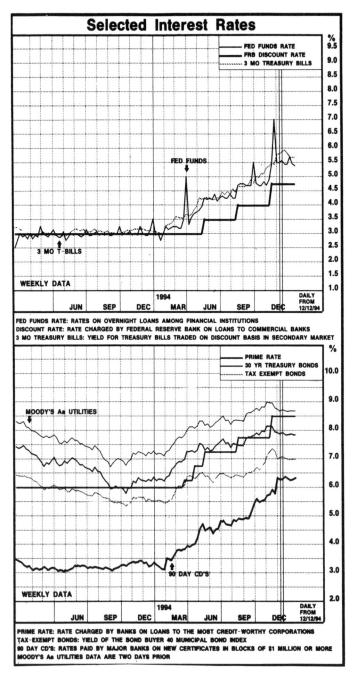

Selected Interest Rates

FED FUNDS RATE
FRB DISCOUNT RATE
3 MO TREASURY BILLS

FED FUNDS

3 MO T-BILLS

WEEKLY DATA

JUN   SEP   DEC   1994 MAR   JUN   SEP   DEC   DAILY FROM 12/12/94

FED FUNDS RATE: RATES ON OVERNIGHT LOANS AMONG FINANCIAL INSTITUTIONS
DISCOUNT RATE: RATE CHARGED BY FEDERAL RESERVE BANK ON LOANS TO COMMERCIAL BANKS
3 MO TREASURY BILLS: YIELD FOR TREASURY BILLS TRADED ON DISCOUNT BASIS IN SECONDARY MARKET

PRIME RATE
30 YR TREASURY BONDS
TAX EXEMPT BONDS

MOODY'S Aa UTILITIES

90 DAY CD'S

WEEKLY DATA

JUN   SEP   DEC   1994 MAR   JUN   SEP   DEC   DAILY FROM 12/12/94

PRIME RATE: RATE CHARGED BY BANKS ON LOANS TO THE MOST CREDIT-WORTHY CORPORATIONS
TAX-EXEMPT BONDS: YIELD OF THE BOND BUYER 40 MUNICIPAL BOND INDEX
90 DAY CD'S: RATES PAID BY MAJOR BANKS ON NEW CERTIFICATES IN BLOCKS OF $1 MILLION OR MORE
MOODY'S Aa UTILITIES DATA ARE TWO DAYS PRIOR

indicators. Among these are the total of time savings deposits, 90-day Treasury Bill yield, brokers' cash accounts, amount of workers' real earnings, brokers margin credit, gold prices, bond yield/prime rate ratio, stock market average PE ratio, and the U.S. federal deficit.

Financial newspapers report a myriad of banking, production, employment, purchasing, and inventory indicators. The tables in Charts 7 and 8 appeared in *Investor's Business Daily*.

Chart 8

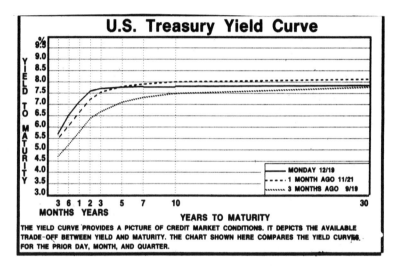

IRA (INDIVIDUAL RETIREMENT ACCOUNT) Before the recent tax law, every astute investor should have realized IRA's were excellent investment vehicles for building or supplementing retirement funds. By setting up an IRA, an individual could knock off up to $2,000 of his annual taxable income besides realizing tax deferred capital appreciation. Congress put an end to this best-of-both-worlds situation with its recent tax reform legislation. But don't count the IRA out. Many people still qualify for tax deductions, and the tax deferral on investment gains in IRAs is still available to all. You can make non-deductible contributions to your IRA and benefit from this continued deferral of taxes.

Tax-free interest compounding yields substantial benefits. For example, $2,000 invested annually with interest compounded daily at 10% will accumulate $134,252 in twenty years. The numbers are even more dramatic if you stash away $2,000 annually at 12% for 25 years. Under this scenario, your tax-sheltered retirement nestegg will grow to $337,437.

Many financial institutions have taken pains to develop and provide IRA guidelines and booklets describing the new rules, in many cases giving easy-to-follow examples. IRS Publication 590, "Tax Information on Individual Retirement Arrangements," also provides detailed but clear information for establishing your IRA options.

According to the Investment Company Institute, an investment industry association for the distribution of investment information, nearly 90 percent of all U.S. households remain eligible for either a partial or full deduction of their IRA contribution in the current tax year.

There are exceptions to the active participant rule with phase out ranges up to $50,000 of adjusted gross income. Obtain the IRA publication and determine whether or not you are still eligible to make tax-deductible IRA contributions. If so, then continuing your IRA is most likely top priority.

Other major rule changes—you can now purchase state coins or U.S. minted gold and silver coins of one ounce or less; however you may not invest in collectibles such as stamps, antiques, rugs, metals or guns.

The traditional IRA investment, and one that is still very popular, has been the certificate of deposit (CD). CDs offer a guaranteed rate over a fixed period of time with relatively little risk. Different maturity periods can fit almost any IRA time frame. Bank CDs are insured by the FDIC and are one of the safest investments around. The benefits of liquidity and safety are partially offset by poor protection against potential inflation. With locked-in interest rates, inflation erodes a CD's value. Even so, CDs can form a valuable portion of a conservative IRA or one to be closed or reduced in the near future due to pending retirement or other circumstances.

Another investment vehicle suitable for conservative investors and those nearing retirement is the money market fund. It offers safety, liquidity, and an interest rate that reflects the actions of the market rate, thereby offering protection from inflation.

By employing a self-directed IRA, *you* maintain the control over where your contributions are invested. This gives you the flexibility to switch portions of your portfolio between different types of investments which perform better than other types of investments in certain market, interest rate, and economic scenarios. For example, gold investments tend to outperform interest sensitive investments like long-term bonds during periods of rapid inflation. On the other hand, stocks and bonds may outperform gold when the economy is strong and inflation held in check.

Using a self-directed IRA account provides you with diversification capabilities. If you invested all your IRA capital in certificates of deposit, you run the risk that interest rates will rise substantially and leave you with a below par return on your money. Likewise, if you invested totally in a money market mutual fund and interest rates started to drop, your yield would decline in conjunction with the interest rates.

Treasury obligations and zero-coupon bonds are other ways to lock in interest rates. Zeros sell at deep discounts, and the interest rate is fixed until the bond matures at face value. Since interest is taxed on an annual basis, zeros are ideal investments for an IRA's tax deferred status. Corporate zeros can have substantially higher interest rates, but remember the risk factor.

Investment in individual stocks offers dividend earnings, capital appreciation, and plenty of excitement. Utility stocks used to be considered investments for grandmothers, but recent events make them worthy IRA picks. Decreasing construction expenditures have made cash cows of many utilities looking for alternative business investments.

Of course, some carry significant nuclear exposure, and others have cost overruns from previous plant construction activities that have yet to be settled with the public utility commissions.

Innovative utility managements have embarked on profitable diversification efforts under their holding company umbrellas. New business lines include purchasing of regional banks, joint ventures with specialized paper manufacturers, and alternative energy source ventures.

All in all, there are plenty of solid, well-run utility companies that offer attractive yields and the opportunity to participate in the rise in their stock price.

For investors who want a "double play," convertibles are hybrid securities that pay interest or dividends at a given rate but participate in the appreciation of the underlying common stock through the convertible feature. The convertible bond or convertible preferred stock investor can lock in a decent yield while maintaining the ability to achieve capital appreciation should the common stock price rise.

If you wish to invest in stocks and bonds but lack the time, expertise or disposition, you can choose from a vast array of IRA mutual funds. There is a mutual fund to match every conceivable investment philosophy. Diversified mutual funds spread their investment assets over different securities and industries. Specialty funds offer a concentrated approach to investing. Some invest in only gold companies, others in U.S. government bonds, while still others ferret out emerging growth companies.

Mutual funds provide professional investment management to the small investor through the pooling of funds. Unfortunately, professional and profitable management do not always coincide. Some mutuals perform better in up markets, while others shine in bear markets. Look carefully at past performances over different time frames (six months, one year, three years, five years) and in relation to the market performance overall. Another caveat—make sure you understand the fee structure before you buy.

Remember, there are still plenty of opportunities, regardless of the tax law changes, for tax-deferred investment gains through IRAs. Plenty of fine investments exist, but review their progress in relation to your investment goals. Play an active part in your investments. Don't just buy a security or mutual fund and forget about it. Your retirement future depends upon your active and informed involvement. Contribute to your IRA and invest wisely.

INVESTMENT CLUB An investment club is a partnership of investors pooling their resources to make security purchases based on a consensus of opinion. Investment clubs serve many purposes. In some instances, they function as a social outlet, while in other instances the investment club is strictly for the business of investing.

Besides pooling their cash resources, investment club members pool their investment knowledge as well as increase the number of investment alternatives that can be investigated in a given period of time.

With over 30,000 investment clubs in existence, up substantially from only 15,000 in 1980, investment clubs are fast becoming an important factor in the market.

Investors are attracted to investment clubs for several reasons. First of all, the low monthly cash outlay is affordable by almost all potential investors. Second, the pooling of resources allows an investor to participate in a much boarder range of investments. Finally, investment club meetings provide education on different investment philosophies and alternatives.

Generally, investment clubs follow the dollar cost averaging strategy of investing. Dollar cost averaging depends on regular investment of a fixed number of dollars in a specific stock or portfolio of stocks. Market timers depend on judgement as to when to buy or sell, while dollar cost investors buy regularly, accumulating more shares when prices are down and less shares when prices have risen.

The method eliminates the uncertainty of market timing and the risk of being out of the market at an inopportune time and missing profit opportunities. Although dollar cost averaging is used by individuals and investment clubs, it is not for the timid. The investor must not lose faith and stop buying during a bear market. The purpose of dollar cost averaging is to acquire shares at an average price that would be lower than if the shares were purchased at once through market timing.

Besides using dollar cost averaging by belonging to an investment club, an individual investor can try the strategy through company savings plans, individual stock purchases, and dividend reinvestment programs.

There are many group benefits to be derived from establishing a new investment club or joining an existing club. Clubs offer a unique way to gain investment experience and knowledge while keeping a lid on the anxiety level.

Considerable truth rests in the old saying, "There is safety in numbers." Investment clubs reflect this adage because they offer the opportunity to discuss and debate investment decisions. This feature allows you to draw on the accumulated investment experience and expertise of others, possibly saving you from an investment disaster that could set your financial planning back years. In addition, your investment club partners help acquaint you with different investment philosophies and strategies. Remember, membership provides you with access to more investigative minds which can evaluate a larger and more diverse range of investments than you could cover on your own.

The benefits are not solely restricted to stock picking. Although the main purpose of the investment club remains to better educate its members on the stock market, many clubs invite noted authorities on other financial topics to speak at club meetings. The experts don't have to be of national stature to be informative and interesting. Many local and regional speakers on financial topics can provide plenty for your club members to learn and consider for their own financial situation. For example, tax experts and financial planners can discuss ways to cut the inheritance tax burden with various estate trust arrangements. The National Association of Investment Clubs located at 711 West Thirteen Mile Road, Madison Heights, MI 48071, 810-583-6242, is a non-profit organization dedicated to the education of the individual investor and investment club members.

The association provides advice on starting up investment clubs, provides a number of investment tools and manuals, and publishes an investment newsletter highlighting attractive stock investments.

NAIC promotes an investment philosophy based on regular investment regardless of market conditions, dividend and capital gain reinvestment, purchase of growth stocks, and investment in different industries and company sizes.

The American Association for Individual Investors (AAII) represents another source of investment information for club members and individual investors. Its members number in excess of 100,000. The group sponsors investment seminars on a regular basis across the country and provides members with other investment literature such as the AAII's "Journal" published 10 times a year. For information write to AAII at 625 North Michigan Avenue, Chicago, Illinois 60611 or call (312) 280-0170. Other membership attractions include discounts on investment software and financial publications such as *Barron's, Investor's Business Daily, Business Week,* and *Fortune,* free Standard & Poor's reports on a large number of companies, eligibility for special money market account, and special AAII Gold Mastercard privileges.

When starting an investment club, it is extremely important to clearly define the responsibilities of each club member in order to prevent disagreements and misunderstandings further down the road. Agree upon a regular time and place for regular meetings. While the club should be fun as well as profitable, assuming a businesslike approach to club meetings will pay dividends in the long run. Set up rules for entering and leaving club membership, determine a method for portfolio valuation, and agree upon a policy for dividend distributions.

Establish a speaker's program to expand members' knowledge on a wide range of financial topics that can benefit members both in their club investment and in their own personal financial planning efforts. The club also needs to address the safe guarding of stocks and whether or not to register them in the club's name, the name of a bonded officer or in "street name" with the club's broker. Perhaps most important, the club's overall investment strategy and philosophy needs to be agreed upon in advance of any investment decision making.

Many clubs spread the duties equally among club members on a rotating basis so each gets to participate in all aspects of running the club. The committee approach is another popular method. To illustrate, half of your members could serve on the stock selection committee, which decides on new purchases, while the other half serves on the portfolio committee, which monitors current stock holdings and decides when to sell or buy more. These approaches help keep everybody active in the club and the meetings lively and informative for all concerned.

Search out a stock broker who can provide the level of service and information you desire at competitive commission rates. Uncle Sam requires that each club obtain a tax identification number and file appropriate tax forms. If a club is a partnership, most clubs form as partnerships, the members must report their share of profits or losses on individual tax returns.

Investment clubs can be used to fund IRAs but the investment club bylaws must specifically allow IRA accounts.

The following four investment principles will help spur your club's growth:

1.   Invest a set sum once a month in common stocks, regardless of market conditions. This helps you obtain lower average costs.

2.   Reinvest dividends and capital gains immediately. Your money grows faster if earnings are reinvested. This is compounding at work.

3.   Buy growth stocks, companies whose sales are increasing at a faster rate than for the industry in general. The companies should have good prospects for continued growth.

4.   Invest in different fields. Diversification helps spread risk and present opportunities for gains.

MARGIN Margin is the use of brokers' funds to purchase additional securities. An investor must deposit enough equity in his account to purchase shares on margin. Margin requirements are regulated by Federal Reserve Regulation T. It can be used effectively to leverage investments, thus increasing overall return on investment.

Under margin rules, you can borrow money from your broker to purchase stocks. Certainly, your broker is not going to give you free access to his personal checking account—Federal Reserve Regulation T establishes the minimum percentage a broker may accept to cover the purchase or short sale of a stock.

Margin requirements have ranged from 50 to 80% in recent years, currently resting at 50%. In effect, you can purchase twice the amount of stock with the same amount of money or the same amount of stock with only half. Another bonus—you can still deduct the interest from your taxable income, assuming your net investment gain exceeds the margin interest charge. Investors can borrow from their brokers on margin by placing securities or cash as collateral for the margin loan. In addition to the Federal Reserve 50% margin requirement, the New York Stock Exchange has a minimum

$2000 initial equity requirement. Keep in mind that brokers will not accept stock that trades below $10 a share as collateral.

All brokerage margin customers are required to sign margin agreements that spell out the terms of the loan and other requirements of the margin agreement. Remember, the brokerage firm is legally bound to have its customers maintain certain margin requirements. The margin agreement details what actions may be taken to get the account back within acceptable margin limits.

Margins are constantly monitored by the brokerage firm. When the margin gets low, the broker sends out a "margin call" letter similar to the following:

"Due to recent market action and in accordance with federal margin regulations, it will be necessary for you to deposit with our firm as soon as possible, but in any event before (date), the sum of (amount), (or acceptable securities having a loan value of at least that amount)."

The margin call may also be in the form of a telegram or telephone call, but the message is the same—send money.

If you fail to make the margin call, your security positions may be sold to satisfy the margin shortfall. Your losses could be substantial if your stock holdings are liquidated, even though the downturn in your stock portfolio might prove to be temporary. Guard against this possibility by maintaining your margin and responding promptly to margin calls. Make sure you have adequate cash reserves or borrowing capacity to meet any anticipated margin calls.

Obviously, one risk of trading on margin is that you may be forced to sell at the wrong time. Another risk is that you might overextend yourself and purchase more investments than are prudent for your financial condition. Remember, leverage works both ways. Your investment losses will mount twice as fast if the price declines in the stocks you pick.

Brokerage houses also have their own policies, called house maintenance requirements and maintenance margin, which set additional minimum equity levels for customer margin accounts. Now, if you haven't been frightened off by potential margin pitfalls, let's take a look at how margin can be used to your advantage.

First of all, as mentioned earlier, investment interest is fully deductible as long as it does not exceed your net investment income. Interest on margin loans vary from broker to broker so it pays to shop around. Brokers tie their margin interest fees to the broker call rate—the rate at which the brokerage borrows from its capital source.

The second and major advantage of margin investing is the substantial leverage available. To illustrate, assume you have $25,000 to invest. You have been following the fortunes of XYZ Inc. and believe its business will grow substantially in the future, driving up its stock price. Ignoring commissions, at a price of $25 per share you can purchase 1,000 shares of XYZ. If the stock jumps $2.50 a share, your profit will be $2,500 or 10% of your original investment—a tidy gain to reward your astute stock picking.

However, using 50% margin, you could have purchased 2,000 shares of XYZ for the same $25,000 investment. The $2.50 share price rise would now translate into a $5,000 gain, or a 20% return in investment profits, which is double the return on your investment without margin. The differences between the two accounts are the interest costs to trade on margin and the degree of risk associated with holding twice as much stock during a downturn in the market or your stock holdings.

You can minimize the margin interest by investing in stocks with dividends that will help offset the margin interest charges. A well-balanced portfolio of stocks in your margin account, as in your other accounts, can provide a measure of safety against margin calls due to a drop in any one or two of your stocks.

Trading on margin offers substantial benefits if it fits your financial position and investment disposition.

MOVING AVERAGE The moving average of a security is calculated by adding the new price, dropping off the old price, and dividing by the number of days in the period. Moving averages are followed to determine the price direction of a particular security, group of stocks, commodities, or the market in general.

Chart 9

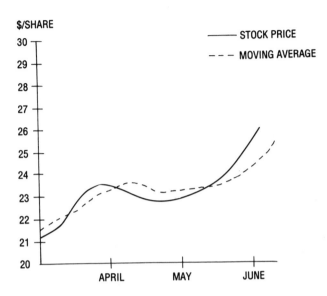

NEGATIVE YIELD CURVE An abnormal condition in investment markets when short-term interest rates are higher than
long-term rates.

Chart 10

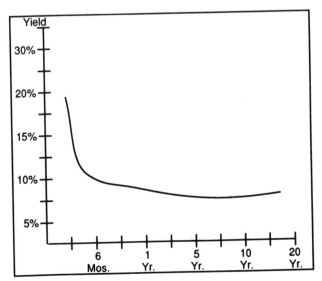

ODD BALL THEORIES Everybody knows they're not worth a tinker's damn, but come the second week of January when the National Football League (NFL) team beats the American Football League (AFL) contender in the Super Bowl, we all rest easy, secure in the knowledge that the market will rise for yet another year.

"The Super Bowl Stock Market Theory" originated in 1979 as a diversion from my more serious work. While there's obviously no real connection to the stock market, "I've created a financial Frankenstein because of its track record," says chief Super Bowl pundit, Robert H. Stovall, president of Stovall/Twenty-First Advisers, Inc. in New York.

Indeed, the uncanny accuracy of Stovall's theory spawned a number of Super Bowl investment formulas published by a variety of people. In the world of stock market theories, as in its real world counterpart, success has a thousand fathers and failure none.

Simply put, the theory espouses that when the Super Bowl is played in January, the market will close higher if the game is won by an "original" NFC team, but decline if the game is won by a team from the AFL.

There is more to the theory than meets the eye. It is loaded statistically: there are more NFL teams since the original NFC teams such as Cleveland, Pittsburgh, and the Colts (wherever they happen to be currently domiciled) are now counted as NFL teams. In addition, markets tend to go up more years than they go down.

Football has nothing over on baseball. Consider the infallible (to date) New York Mets Market Reverse Market Indicator.

Everytime the Mets have played in the World Series, the market has taken a tumble the next year. For example, in 1969, the Mets won their first World Series in five games over Baltimore and the market plummeted to 724.33 on April 28, 1970, the lowest point since November 22, 1963, when President Kennedy was shot. The Mets next appeared in the 1973 World Series, losing to Oakland in seven games. In 1974, the S&P, impacted by the failure of Franklin National Bank, largest bank failure in history up to that time, posted a 26.5 percent retreat. The Mets were Series bound again in 1986 and we all know about the minor technical correction in October 1987.

Don't invest your track winnings in the stock market after your favorite horse captures the Triple Crown. Triple Crown winners spell bad omens for the market. In eight of the 11 years since 1919 in which the same horse won the Kentucky Derby, the Preakness and the Belmont States, the Dow posted a net low for the year.

It all started with Assault, the 1946 Triple Crown winner. That year, the Dow backtracked 8.1 percent. Two years later, jockey Eddie Arcaro guided Citation through the three victories, nosing the Dow down 2.1 percent. In 1973, Secretariat took the honors, plunging the Dow another 16.6 percent. Then in 1977, Seattle Slew slew the market average by 17.3 percent. Finally, Affirmed won the most recent Triple Crown. The market appeared unimpressed and declined a modest 3.1 percent.

While the Triple Crown Theory indeed appears ominous, there is a consolation prize of sorts. If a horse wins the first two races but bites the dust in the Belmont Stakes, the Dow finishes higher nearly 70 percent of the time.

Speaking of superstitions, brings Friday the 13th to mind. Back in 1986, two University of Miami professors set aside their research on black cats and studied the effect of Friday the 13th on the stock market. They discovered that stock prices fell on an average annual rate of 24.5 percent on Friday the 13ths from 1962 to 1985, signifying that strong elements were at work because other theories hold Fridays to be strong up days, with an average annual increase of 27.9 percent.

If you think one Friday the 13th is bad enough, then research on years in which 3 Friday the 13ths occur will make you shake in your investment boots.

There have been six years with 3 Friday the 13ths over the past 40 years. A recession stated in three of those years and an economic contraction in two others. In 1984, a recession didn't materialize but economic growth slowed considerably. We all know what happened in October 1987.

The next year with 3 Friday the 13ths doesn't occur until 1998.

Everywhere you look, theories to predict stock market behavior abound. Try these on for size: if hemlines rise, so will stocks; high coiffure styles signal market tops; the weekend effect results in lower stock prices on Mondays; Presidential election years bode well for the market; companies with letter names, such as XYZ, perform worse than their industry counterparts; and the fifth year of a decade pushes up stock prices.

For my part, I don't believe in these theories, I subscribe to my own scientific treatise—whenever the line in front of the quote machine at the local brokerage office extends beyond five people, I sell all my stock and whenever the line only holds two people I buy everything I can get my hands on.

OPTION The following glossary of option terms should prove to be a handy reference.

At The Money When the market price of the underlying security is equal to the exercise price of the option, it is said to the "at the money."

Call The right to purchase a specific security at a specified price for a specified time period.

Closing Transaction A transaction prior to expiration of the option when the buyer of an option makes an offsetting purchase of an identical option. The closing transaction cancels out an investor's previous option position.

Covered Call A call option sold by a writer who owns the underlying security.

Expiration Date The date when the option expires. If the option has not been exercised prior to the expiration date, it expires worthless. Options on common stocks expire on the Saturday following the third Friday of the expiration month.

Exercise Price The price at which the buyer of a call option has the right to purchase the underlying security or the buyer of a put option has the right to sell the underlying security.

In The Money An option whose underlying security market price is such that the option has intrinsic value. An option is "in the money" if the current market price is higher than the striking price of a call option or lower than the striking price of a put option.

Intrinsic Value If the option gives the right to buy a specific stock at less than its current market value or the right to sell a specific stock at more than its current market value, it is said to have intrinsic value.

Naked Value Any option that the buyer or seller does not have covered with an underlying security position.

Opening Transaction A purchase or sale which results in an investor becoming either the buyer or writer of an option.

Put The right to sell a specific security at a specified price for a specified time period.

Striking Price See *Exercise Price* above.

Time Value When an option has no intrinsic value, its premium is a function of the amount of time left to create intrinsic value.

Underlying Security The security which must be delivered upon exercise of an option.

Writer An investor that sells an option and earns a premium. The writer is obligated to deliver the underlying security in the case of a call option or to purchase the underlying security in the case of a put option.

PENNY STOCKS Penny stocks have always attracted investors hoping to make a killing in the stock market. Traded via the "pink sheets" and in the over-the-counter (OTC) system, and costing less than a dollar a share in many cases, penny stocks are among the longest of long shots in financial markets.

The low prices of pennies are their main attraction. The chance to hit that "big one" that rises from 20 cents to $20 a share can easily outweigh the risks of dozens of losers.

Probably more than any other area, penny stocks conjure up a mirror image of what businesses or industries are the current hot growth prospects.

For example, a rise in the price of gold spawns a new generation of exploration and mining companies seeking their fortunes in bullion or other exotic minerals. The energy crunches of the 1970s and early 1980s led to successive waves of new oil and gas exploration and drilling companies. Likewise, start-up firms in computer hardware and software, solar technology, genetic engineering and biotechnology, and every other industrial trend have exploited the penny stock markets to raise capital for research, product development, and expansion.

Since the prospects of many new penny stocks rising to lofty stock prices are rather dismal, penny stock investing is not for the fainthearted. You will most likely have to endure innumerable disappointments while searching for a hot company with a real future. Information is often scant regarding the fledgling companies that start their lives on the pink sheets or over-the-counter markets.

Actually, if you understand at the outset that you're looking for true long shots, and you decide going in how much money you are going to risk, you can have a lot of fun with penny stocks. Tolerating the string of weak performers that will surround the winners is a matter of attitude; don't take it too seriously. If nothing else, such a viewpoint will help you to sleep at night.

No matter how you pursue penny stocks, good information is essential for prudent decisions. Some university and public libraries carry a selection of penny market newsletters and other reference material. In addition, numerous penny stockbrokers will happily send you information, and a number of advisory services are available at a wide range of prices.

Keep yourself informed on the companies and their respective industries. New events will make certain companies or industries more attractive. For example, leaching, a major technological improvement in gold mining, has significantly reduced the cost of gold recovery. Particularly for struggling companies, such a development can mean the difference between profitability and bankruptcy.

One strategy of penny stock investing calls for investing regularly in penny stocks. Decide how much you can afford to put at risk with pennies and invest it. Regular participation will keep you on top of your speculations.

Denver is the traditional heart of the penny stock business. In the 1880s, penny stock arrived in the Colorado city as a way to finance silver and gold exploration—early mining pioneers found that they could raise their needed capital more easily if they sold many low-priced shares, rather than a smaller number at higher prices. Thus, the use of penny stocks to fund mineral exploration is not new. The theory carries over into almost any risky venture in a new area, such as the shale oil ventures during the energy crisis, drug and medical research companies, advanced laser technology, and so on.

In most cases, the term "penny stocks" has fallen victim to inflation. Pennies used to be any stock priced below $1 a share, but now stocks under $5 a share are termed pennies. In any event, the price is relatively low, the risk is high, and the rewards for the occasional success stories can be great.

Since early mining efforts gave birth to penny stocks, the mining industry is as good a place as any to use for an example. As we mentioned earlier, the use of cyanide leaching techniques is creating a new gold rush in Nevada and other Western states. Leaching methods cost $1 per ton of ore, as opposed to $4 per ton in conventional ore processing. And leaching operations can recover gold at less than $200 per ounce, which means most operations can maintain prices in gold price downturns.

One company that inched its way out of the penny stock realm and back is U.S. Gold Corporation (USGL) (formerly Silver State Mining Company). U.S. Gold stock's price rose from a low of 25 cents a share in 1982 to a high of $3.625 a share in early 1987 before tumbling to 31 cents a share in late 1990 and rebounding to 62 1/2 cents a share in mid-1993 before declining again.

If you focus on mining stocks such as U.S. Gold, then you should read the various mining journals that focus on the industry—the publications are filled with interesting articles on the mining industry and its companies. The same is true for almost every industry area of specialization you might explore, such as biotechnology, medical technology, computer hardware and software, franchising, etc.

Pentech International Inc. represents a penny stock success story. A 1985 startup, Pentech's stock traded as low as 3/8 before hitting an all time high of 9 7/8 in 1992. An investment of $1,000 for 2,000 shares when the stock traded at 1/2 could have been sold in 1992 for $19,750, not a bad investment return. The brainchild of Norman Melnick, an industry legend who developed the quick-dry ink systems for ball point pens and the first low-cost market pen with non-toxic ink, Pentech continues to carve out a profitable niche in the pen and drawing instrument market.

Many small companies in biotechnologies and medical research are generating some major technological breakthroughs. Takeovers by larger firms with the funds to capitalize on the research results can make a small research company's stock an instant winner.

If you decide to participate in penny stocks, remember not to get caught up in the speculative fever that occurs during bull markets. Investigate the company and its industry before investment and make informed decisions.

Over the years, penny stock swindles and swindlers have made their way into the headlines of the nation's newspapers. For instance, the Securities and Exchange commission (SEC) and the National Association of Securities Dealers, Inc. (NASD) routinely levied fines and placed other sanctions on some penny stock brokerage firms for overcharging and misleading investors in thinly traded "pink sheet" stocks underwritten by the company.

It is clear that investors should take adequate precautions to make sure the companies they invest in are reputable and financially solid. Don't let the fact that a firm is listed on an exchange lull you into a false sense of security. As with any investment, dabbling in penny stocks requires an analysis of the firm's finances, management, track record, industry and prospects.

The SEC provides three warning signs of penny stock fraud. First comes an unsolicited phone call, often promising quick profits with little or no risk. Remember, if an investment opportunity sounds too good to be true, it probably is. Second, the caller uses high pressure sales tactics eluding to "inside" information, unique opportunities available only for a short time or linkages of the purchase of a particular stock only if you also agree to buy stock of another company. Third, a strong resistance on the part of the penny stock broker to sell your stock for cash.

The key is to investigate before you invest. If you can not get detailed information about the company, don't invest. Inquire about the penny stock broker's company. Request all information in writing. Ask how long the firm has been in business. Your state's Division of Securities Regulation or local office of the NASD can determine if the firm and salesperson are licensed to do business in your state.

Finally, if you suspect fraud or cannot resolve your conflict with a penny stock broker contact your state's Division of Securities Regulation, Securities and Exchange Commission, Office of Consumers Affairs and Information Services, 450 Fifth Street, N.W., Washington, D.C. 20549-0001 or the NASD Surveillance Department, 1735 K Street, N.W., Washington, D.C. 20006-1516.

Penny stock issues do offer unique investment opportunities but you must tread carefully.

POINT AND FIGURE CHART The point and figure chart consists of plotting prices over a given period, not in the form of a continuous line, but by a series of x's and o's. Prices are rounded off to whole numbers. For example, closing prices of 25 1/4, 25 1/8, 25 3/4 and 25 3/8 would all be plotted as prices of 25. In this way, the price ignores minor fluctuations and concentrates on major price movements.

X's indicate upward price movements while o's indicate downward price movements. Each time a price direction changes, a new column is used to track movement. The resulting pattern of x's and o's reflects the security's ability to sustain an upward or downward price movement.

Chart 11

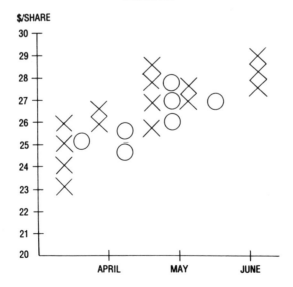

PUT OPTION A put option provides the holder the right to sell a specific security at a specified period of time. Put options are purchased with the anticipation that the underlying stock will decrease in value in excess of the premium paid for the put. When this happens, the holder can sell the put for a higher price or can exercise the option and purchase the stock at the lower current market price for delivery at the higher exercise price (normally the put itself is sold for a gain rather than incur commissions on the purchase of the stock). The effective use of puts can result in a highly leveraged gains.

An investor can be either a writer of an option or a purchaser (holder). The premium is the price set by the market and varies according to changes in the marketplace of the underlying stock, amount of time left in the option period, and volatility of the underlying security. For instance, if the price of the underlying security tends to fluctuate in a wide range, then the option premium will command a higher price. In general, the longer the option has to run, the higher the premium will be in relation to similar options with shorter time frames before expiration. The investor can buy puts with the intent of making a profit on the decline of the underlying stock. For example, a purchase of a put on XYZ, Inc. at a strike price of 10 can be purchased for 3/16 with an expiration date of October. The listing in the Listed Option Quotations page of financial journals would look like this:

Chart 12

Option & NY Close	Strike Price	Calls—Last			Puts—Last		
		Sep	Oct	Dec	Sep	Oct	Dec
XYZ	10	1 5/16	r	2	r	3/16	r
11 3/8	12 1/2	1/16	5/16	3/4	1	1 3/8	1 7/8
11 3/8	15	r	1/16	3/8	r	3 3/4	r
11 3/8	17 1/2	r	r	3/16	r	6 1/4	r
11 3/8	20	r	1/16	1/16	r	r	r

R = not traded

The XYZ puts with strike prices of 12 1/2, 15, 17 1/2 and 20 are said to be "in the money" which means that at the current XYZ stock market price of 11 3/8, the put has intrinsic value.

Puts can be effective in bearish markets or markets that exhibit a see-saw action providing both up and down opportunities.

Using the information on XYZ, the following examples illustrate some basic put strategies. (Commission will be ignored on all examples to keep the calculations simple.)

EXAMPLE 1: Assume that you believe that XYZ stock will go below 10 before the expiration date of the October put. A purchase of 10 puts will give you the option to sell 1,000 shares of XYZ stock at $10 per share. The cost of purchasing the 10 puts is $187.50 ($.1875 x 1,000); this is called the option premium. A drop in the price of XYZ to $9 a share before your October puts expire will result in a gain of $812.50 ($1 below strike price x 1,000 shares less $187.50 option premium), more than quadrupling your original investment.

EXAMPLE 2: You may already own 500 shares of XYZ stock and it will be a good investment in the long run. In this case, you may want to protect against any downside risk by purchasing a put which will increase in value as the stock declines, thereby helping to offset your XYZ stock holdings.

Your current holdings are worth $5,687.50 (500 shares at $11.375). Assume you purchase 5 October puts with a strike price of 10 for 3/16. The premium will cost you $93.75 ($.1875 x 500). A drop in the price of XYZ stock to $8 a share before your October puts expire will result in a loss in stock value of $1687.60 ($3.375 drop in price x 500 shares), but a gain of $906.25 ($2 below stock price x 500 shares less $93.75 premium) will offset over half of the decline in stock value. The matching of put purchases with stock holdings can help offset stock price declines.

Puts offer inexpensive strategies to gain on price declines or protect current holdings—but there is risk involved. An investor may be wrong about the direction of the expected price change, the magnitude of the price change, or the timing of the price change. Any one of these failed expectations can result in the put option expiring worthless.

In addition to buying put options, an investor can also write put options. In this case, the writer of the option is obligated to purchase shares of the underlying security at the strike price if the put is exercised by the purchaser. The obligation continues until the option expiration date. Investors write put options to earn premium income when they believe the price of the underlying stock will remain steady within a narrow range or will rise during the option period.

To insure that the stock can be purchased in case the put is exercised, the put writer must deposit and maintain adequate funds with his broker. In the event the writer would like to terminate his obligation before expiration date, the writer can purchase an identical put at the then current price. This, in effect, liquidates his position and the profit or loss is the difference between the premium received for writing the put and the premium paid for purchasing the identical put.

There are more intricate strategies involving more risk, but a conservative investor can make profitable use of puts using the basic strategies outlined above. To obtain more information on puts, contact your broker. Most investment firms and The Chicago Board Options Exchange (CBOE) provide option literature that explains the basics of options, illustrated with easy to understand examples.

Options are traded on several exchanges such as the Chicago Board of Options, American Exchange, and Philadelphia Exchange.

For a glossary of option terms refer to *Option* in Section II.

RETURN There are various financial methods for measuring and comparing return from investment alternatives. A brief discussion of the more well-known methods follows.

RETURN ON INVESTMENT (ROI) Return on investment is a financial management tool designed to measure both past performance and future investment decision alternatives. ROI searches out the best investment alternative that will maximize economic earnings contributed to the organization.

ROI correlates the business investment in capital assets to the firm's output of goods and services. The ROI formula stresses the relationships between profits and sales, and sales and investment in assets:

$$ROI = \frac{Profit}{Sales} \times \frac{Sales}{Assets}$$

RETURN ON EQUITY (ROE) Return on equity is the percentage earned on a firm's common stock equity and measures the profitability of the company in relation to the amount of stockholder's common stock equity.

$$ROE = \frac{Period\ Net\ Income}{Common\ Stock\ Equity}$$

RETURN ON INVESTED CAPITAL (ROIC) Return on invested capital measures the profitability in relation to the total capital of the company, both common and preferred stock equity plus long-term funded debt.

$$ROIC = \frac{Earnings\ Before\ Int.,\ Tax\ \&\ Div.}{Total\ Capital}$$

REVERSAL Technical analysis term describing a major shift in direction of an investment security or market index. The chart illustrates a reversal occurring around $27 per share market price.

Chart 13

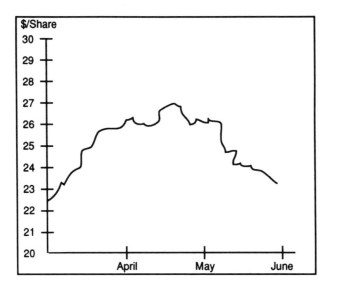

SAUCER A stock or commodity chart pattern resembling a saucer via the formation of a bottom and subsequent price rise. The bottom of the saucer pattern exhibits a support level.

Chart 14

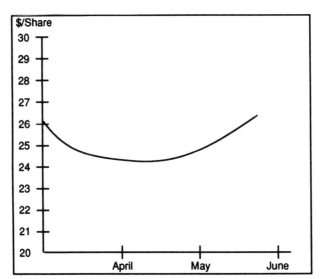

SELLING CLIMAX A drastic plunge in security prices, usually signalling the panic near the end of a bear market. Technicians interpret the selling climax as a buying opportunity in anticipation of a rally that will shortly follow the sharp drop in prices. In the chart, a selling climax begins around 2600 with a sharp recovery beginning around 2300.

Chart 15

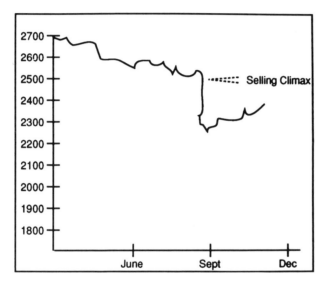

SHORT SALE A short sale is the sale of stock not owned in order to take advantage of an anticipated drop in the stock's market price.

Short sellers believe there is plenty of money to be made on the downside of stock prices, both short-term and long-term. During price runups, short sellers are busy ferreting out stocks that have moved up considerably more than they should have based on their financial expectations. In effect, short selling is betting money that these stock prices will take a tumble.

Short selling strategy does not advocate selling stocks from your portfolio that generate good dividend income or have further price appreciation potential. However, there are money-making opportunities in betting on the price downturn of specific stocks by "selling short."

Short selling philosophy is simple. You sell a stock you think is priced too high (in effect borrowing the stock from your broker) and, in turn, repurchase the stock after the price has fallen to a level that will enable you to recover your commissions and pocket a gain. You are said to be in a short position when you have borrowed shares of stock in order to make a short sale.

There are special rules of which you need to be aware if you plan to participate in the exciting and profitable world of short selling. A short sale may always be made at a price higher than that of the last sale or at the same price of the last sale, if the last proceeding change in the security's price was upward. This is called the "short sale," "uptick," or "plus tick" rule. Therefore, it may take your broker longer to execute a short trade.

In order to sell a stock short, you must put up 50% of the value of the stock you want to short. The collateral can be in the form of cash or securities. This involves setting up a margin account if you do not already have one. It is important to remember that if the stock rises you may be subject to a margin call if the value of your pledged assets falls below 30% of the stock market value (individual brokerage firms may have stricter requirements). Make sure you have plenty of capital or collateral in order to prevent a forced repurchase of your shorted stock at an unfavorable price.

Many investors find it psychologically impossible to use short selling as an effective investment tool. For some, betting against the stock market and good fortunes of American companies is tantamount to treason. Others cannot bring themselves to sell something they do not own. The risk of unlimited loss, since a company stock may continue to rise in value, unnerves many a potential short seller.

For the investor willing to learn some new rules and adapt to some unconventional investment decision processes, short selling offers unique profit opportunities. To illustrate how short selling works, assume that you believe FE Corporation, a fictitious steel manufacturer, is overpriced at its current price of 13 3/8. Its stock has experienced a sharp rise from a low of 4 1/8.

As a follower of the steel industry, you are aware that imports still command a large percentage of steel sales and the return of USX to the steel marketplace after its long strike will put additional pressures on other steel producers. In addition, the bankruptcy of LTV has afforded it court protection and lower labor costs.

Spend some time investigating *Value Line, Standard & Poor's,* and brokerage firm research reports on FE Corporation. Look at its long-term debt position. Follow steel industry production figures. Armed with the results of your investment research, you instruct your broker to short 1,000 share of FE Corporation at 13 3/8. The share price will fall to 11 per share and you will have earned $2,375 (1,000 x 2 3/8), ignoring commissions. If you had already had investment holdings in your margin account worth at least $6,687.50 ($13,375.00 x 50%) you could have made the investment with no additional cash outlay, assuming the price of FE Corporation stock does not rise enough to drop your collateral below market value.

All of the financial and industry information needed to make good short selling decisions is readily available from the public library, a university library, your broker, or the company itself. Although there are no hard and fast short selling strategies, the following points provide some clues while looking for companies to short:

- *Thinly traded stocks.* Avoid short selling stocks that do not have an active market. You may be required to return shares that have been "brokered" when the broker who has loaned them out needs them back.

- *Peaking stocks.* Watch for stocks that have reached new highs and started to retreat. Don't be fooled by a stock just settling back in preparation for another run to a new high.

- *Insider trading.* Corporate officers generally do not like to sell their company holdings, and insider trading could be a tipoff of a pending downturn in corporate earnings and stock prices. On the other hand, an officer may need some money for the tuition payment or the purchase of a luxury item.

- *High price-earnings (P/E) ratio.* Companies with high P/E ratios have farther to fall in the event of an earnings downturn. Compare the PE ratio with other companies in the same industry and the market in general to see if it is overpriced. Read up on general economic trends in the industry that may not have caught up yet with the particular company.

- *Low price-earnings (P/E) ratio.* On the other hand, companies with lower P/Es than other firms in their industry generally retreat faster during an economic downturn and trail during an upturn. In effect, they may well have earned their lower P/Es by substandard performance.

- *Short interest activity.* The short interest activity is reported monthly in *Barron's, Investors' Business Daily* and *The Wall Street Journal*. A substantial short interest position in a stock may indicate that you may already be too late to jump on the short bandwagon. If the stock starts to advance, the large short position could fuel a major advance in the stock's price. Such a rapid price rise forces short investors to cover their short positions by repurchasing the stock and sending the price up further. This is called a short squeeze.

Should the company declare a dividend while you have shorted the stock, you will be required to pay the dividend since the share price is adjusted downward to reflect the dividend payment. As a short seller you do not have to pay margin interest on your shorted position since your broker is not putting up his own funds.

Short selling can also be used to protect a gain in a long position without having to sell the underlying shares. This is referred to as "going short against the box."

Study industry, stock market, and company trends for short selling opportunities.

SPIN-OFF Companies partake in spinning-off corporate units for various reasons. Some operations no longer fit the firm's long-term strategic plans, others need the freedom from rigid big company regulations to be more responsive to the marketplace and others are just plain dogs.

Why would any investor in his right mind invest in spinoff companies when their own parents cut the corporate umbilical cord and sent these orphans out to fend for themselves? On the surface, it's hard to argue with the available negative evidence.

Many orphans operate in dull, boring businesses. They arrive on the market with little fanfare to drum up investor interest. Few, if any, institutions purchase or even follow stock of spinoff companies. In fact, institutions that receive orphan stock in a spinoff distribution often dump the stock in a hurry, putting downward pressure on the stock.

However, for the astute investor willing to spend a little investigation time separating the wheat from the chaff, corporate spinoffs represent a unique opportunity to beat the professionals at their own game and earn significant capital gains.

In many cases, management tries to provide better value to shareholders by exposing the market to hidden assets often overshadowed by larger corporate operations. In addition, many analysts and the market in general do not know how to accurately value conglomerates with diverse operations. In such situations, the parts are worth more than the whole and the spinoff unlocks the additional value.

Often, the discrepancy between the stock price and the spinoff's underlying value reaches significant levels. For example, Burlington Northern, Inc. spunoff its resources segment in July 1988 at a price of $25.50 a share. In less than nine months, the stock more than doubled with rumors of a possible hostile takeover by Pennzoil Company.

Look for clear value signals. The degree of ownership by spinoff management and the corporate parent sometimes signals a potential spinoff bonanza. If they maintain a hefty position, it improves the odds that they foresee attractive market opportunities for the new company.

Take a good, hard look at the spinoff company's management team. Does it have wealth of industry experience capable of making the tough decisions required to keep the company profitable? Can management take advantage of opportunities previously shut off due to restrictive capital spending and corporate policies of a large conglomerate?

Evaluate the industry growth prospects and the firm's relative position in the industry. Remember, even firms in slow growth industries can be cash cows that generate funds for expansion into higher growth businesses. Many times, the parent provides the orphan with an ample cash dowry for acquisitions to grow the company. A failed spinoff causes ill will with shareholders of the parent who received stock and reflects back on the corporate parent, a scenario management wishes to avoid.

Be wary of heavy debt loads, especially for companies in cyclical industries. When the next recession starts, you don't want your fortunes tied to a company with massive interest payments which can trigger a cash crisis.

Check financial publications such as *The Wall Street Journal*, *Investor's Business Daily*, and *Barron's* for company announcements and comments on their implications.

To investigate spinoff opportunities, the company itself represents the best source of information. Ask for copies of press releases, financial statements, and Form 10 (a SEC requirement that gives you a five-year history of the business). These adoption papers will help you choose high return orphans to add to your investment family.

SPLIT A split is a change in the number of authorized and outstanding shares through an amendment to the corporation's charter. The stock you own just split its shares. Are you better off? Not on the surface. A split is simply a proportionate increase in the number of shares outstanding without a similar increase in assets. In other words, a two-for-one split does not change your stake in a company. You still own the same percentage of shares outstanding as you did before. It's like swapping a $20 bill for two tens: You now have two pieces of paper, but your $20 is still only $20. In 1989, splits occurred with 906 of the 2,246 issues listed on the New York Stock Exchange.

Shareholders' equity stays the same as a result of a corresponding change in the par value of all previous authorized shares. Dividends are also adjusted to reflect the stock split.

If stock splits result in the shareholder owning the same proportion of ownership before and after the split, then why do stock splits receive so much investor interest? In strict economic theory, a stock split provides no economic gain to the shareholders, but in real life stocks that have split seem to gain new energy and continue their upward spiral. Let's look as some of the reasons for this perception as well as some stock split research compiled over the years.

Most companies authorize stock splits to make their shares more accessible to the general investing public. An individual investor is usually more willing to purchase 300 shares of a $30 stock than to purchase 100 shares of the same stock selling for $90 a share. The commission charge is spread over more shares, enabling the investor to recoup expenses faster. The lower cost per share will probably also guarantee a stronger market in the stock—which has to prove advantageous to current and future stockholders.

Companies offer splits for other reasons too. For instance, a stock split will broaden the shareholder base, making the company less susceptible to institutional transactions and tender offers. In the case of growth companies, stock splits may be used as dividends to entice shareholders while conserving cash for operational requirements or research and development. Consumer product and service-oriented companies, on the other hand, could view the expanded shareholder base resulting from a stock split as a potential group of new customers.

Finally, some companies split stocks with the goal of gaining a listing on the NYSE or some other stock exchange. Before a company can obtain an NYSE listing, it must have at least one million shares of common stock outstanding.

Regardless of the company's motives, there are some common investor assumptions about stock issues offering splits. First, investors believe higher cash dividends usually accompany or shortly follow a stock split, thereby increasing an investor's earnings yield. Second, investors assume a company's management usually will not split its stock unless it already has good reason to expect improved earnings and higher dividend payments. Third, investors feel that specific stocks have optimum price ranges beyond which stock market price gains are limited. Once a stock's price exceeds that range, a split will bring the price back down, making the investor believe it has a greater potential for gain.

Allowing that at least once and possibly all of these assumptions may be true for a given stock, what implications does this have for investment decision making? Timing obviously becomes a major factor. When is the best time to buy or sell the splitting stock?

According to proponents of the efficient market theory, stock prices move quickly to take account of all publicly available information. Therefore, there should be no advantage to investing in a company shortly after its upcoming stock split has been announced.

To a buy-and-hold investor, the implication of a split is good, even though experts argue among themselves about the short-term impact on the stock's price. Waste Management, a trash-disposal company, split its stock four times in the 1980s. Adjusted for those splits, its price rose from a low of $1.50 a share at the start of the decade to almost $36 at the close. Propelling that advance were price earnings that climbed every year, at a 25% annual rate. Splits didn't make Waste Management more profitable, but they did act as signposts of its phenomenal successes to that point.

Major stock splits are not taxable as dividends. Your tax basis per share for capital gains or losses is adjusted in line with the split. For instance, if you paid $50 a share for 100 shares and a two-for-one split occurs, your adjusted purchase price is $25 per share.

STOCK INDEXES The most closely followed index is the Dow Jones Industrial Average composed of the weighted average of 30 actively traded U.S. corporations, typically the country's blue chip companies. Changes are made to the Dow to reflect stock splits, takeovers, a company going public, or to make the index more representative of the market.

For instance, Owens-Illinois was removed from the Dow in March, 1987 when the company went public. Manville was removed from the index when it filed for bankruptcy protection in 1982.

General Foods was removed from the Dow when it was acquired by Philip Morris in 1985. In addition, Philip Morris was added to the Dow while American Brands was removed to make the index more representative.

The following is a list of current companies comprising the Dow and their major lines of business:

ALLIED SIGNAL—Chemicals, oil and gas, and fibers
ALCOA—Aluminum
AMERICAN EXPRESS—Travel, insurance, investments
AT&T—Telecommunications

BETHLEHEM STEEL—Steel
BOEING—Airplanes and aerospace
CHEVRON—Oil
COCA-COLA—Soft drinks
DuPONT—Chemicals, oil and gas
EASTMAN KODAK—Photographic, chemical products
EXXON—Oil
GENERAL ELECTRIC—Electrical equipment
GENERAL MOTORS—Automotive products
GOODYEAR TIRE—Tires and rubber
IBM—Business machine
INTERNATIONAL PAPER—Paper products
McDONALD'S—Fast food and franchising
MERCK—Drugs and specialty chemicals
3M—Scotch tapes and coated adhesives
NAVISTAR INTERNATIONAL—Medium-to heavy-duty trucks
PHILIP MORRIS—Tobacco, brewing and soft drinks
PRIMERICA—Financial services and retailing
PROCTOR & GAMBLE—Household and personal care
SEARS ROEBUCK—Retail, finance and insurance
TEXACO—Oil
USX—Steel, oil and gas
UNION CARBIDE—Chemicals and plastics
UNITED TECHNOLOGIES—Aircraft engines
WESTINGHOUSE—Electrical equipment
F.W. WOOLWORTH—Variety and discount retail.

In addition to the Dow Jones Industrial Average, there are also Dow Jones averages for transportation and utilities. The transportation index is comprised of 20 major transportation company stocks, while the utility index follows 15 utility stocks.

The following chart from *Investor's Business Daily* illustrates movement in the Dow Jones Industrials.

Chart 16

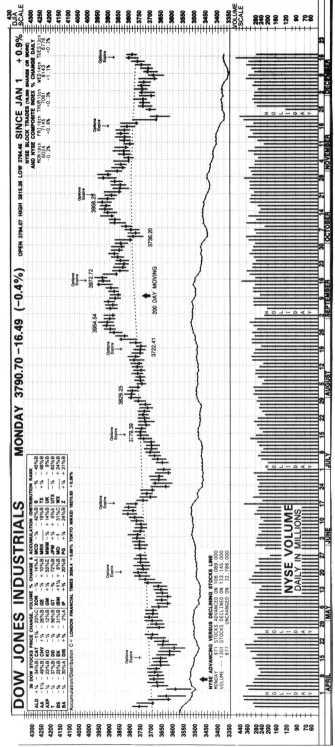

Some indexes are more broad-based than others and may be more representative of the market in general. For example, the S&P 500 is a weighted index of 500 stocks reflecting the aggregate change in market value from the 1941-1943 base period. It represents around 80 percent of the market value of stocks traded on the New York Stock Exchange as well as including some American Exchange and over-the-counter issues.

The S&P 500 is often used as a comparative reference for other market indexes as shown in the chart from *Investor's Business Daily* shown below.

Chart 17

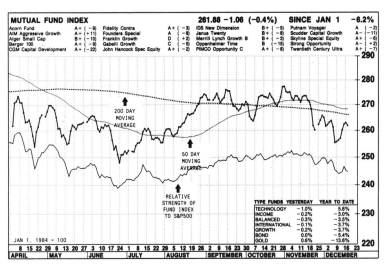

The Wilshire 5000 Equity Index Value weighs all New York Stock Exchange, American Exchange, and over-the-counter stocks making it the broadest stock index. The Wilshire 5000 Index base value reverts back to December 31, 1980

The Value Line Composite Index tracks 1,700 New York Stock Exchange, American Exchange, and over-the-counter stocks using a base value of 100 from June 30, 1961. In contrast to the above indexes, the Value Line Composite is not price or market value weighted.

The following tables, taken from *Investor's Business Daily*, list additional market indexes.

Chart 18

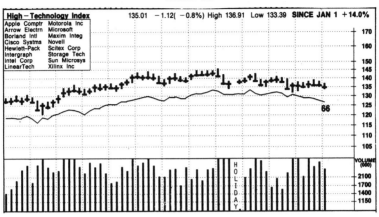

Chart 19

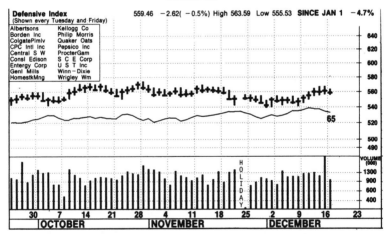

In addition to the stock market indexes, there are any number of other indexes that provide specialized investment information. A particular list includes New York and American Bond Exchange indexes, short-term trading index; the Ryan Index, which is an unweighted average of total return on active Treasury notes and bonds with maturities of two years to thirty years; and the Lipper Convertible Securities Indexes. The NASDAQ Composite Index is a value weighted index of more than 2,000 over the counter issues. With the index's large number of smaller stocks, it is heavily affected by the largest 100 stocks.

Stock indexes are handy investment tools. Many theories are based on the track record of these indexes, some very accurate and others totally false. When making investment decisions, try to interpret the actions of the indexes you follow and their implication for your portfolio. For instance, if your portfolio consists mainly of speculative penny stocks, the movement of the Dow may not mean much to you while, on the other hand, the Wilshire 5000 or the NASDAQ-OTC Price Index probably will.

The importance and influence of stock market indexes is illustrated by the popularity of stock index futures. Stock index future contracts are commitments to buy or sell 500 units of the underlying index for a specified time period. The stock index futures allow investors to speculate on the movement of the market in general or specific sectors of the market as well as providing hedging possibilities for investors in common stocks.

STOP LOSS A stop loss is an order used by investors to protect existing profits or limit losses. The investor instructs the broker to set a sell price for the specific security at a price below the current market price. If the stock price drops to the stop loss price set by the investor, the order becomes a market order thereby allowing the investor to close the position and preserve profits already earned or limit losses.

How many times have you made your investment goal in a company's stock only to have the hard won gains disappear as the stock backslides? Many investors hold on hoping, against hope, that the price decline will be temporary. Unfortunately, more often than not, the price decline negates large portions of gains and sometimes even results in losses.

Stop loss orders provide a simple solution to this investment dilemma. Discipline and the effective use of stop loss orders can help safeguard those profits. Major price gyrations of recent markets (daily as well as weekly) makes it essential that investors know how and when to set stop loss order in action.

A simple example will illustrate how stop loss orders can be beneficial. Suppose you purchase 1,000 shares of AU Corporation, a fictitious gold mining company at $6 a share. Re-

covery in bullion prices along with improved operations have
driven up the price of the stock to $7 3/8 and you have
earned a profit of $1,375 (excluding commission) for a whop-
ping 27.5% return on your investment.

Your analysis of AU Corporation indicates their profit recovery should continue. Gold prices have been distressed and
the fundamentals point to higher bullion prices. You would
like to hold on to your investment but that 27.5% return on
your money looks pretty good.

At this point, you have several choices. First of all, you
can hold onto your AU investment and hope the runup continues. Of course, you risk losing your gain if the stock backslides. Second, you could place a market order and sell your
stock at the best price available, thereby insuring your gains
but forfeiting a chance to participate in further price rises.
Your third choice, setting a stop loss order, offers the benefits
of the first two options: protecting your gains and maintaining
a position in AU Corporation for additional gains. Your stop
loss order can take two forms. A market order stop loss sells
out your shares as soon as the stock hits the specified market
price. If you set a market order stop loss for AU Corporation
at $7.00 a share, your holdings would be put up for sale right
after AU Corporation hits $7.00. The next sale could either be
higher or lower than $7.00 but your shares will be sold out re-
gardless. The fact that the price of AU Corporation reaches or
passes the specified stop prices does not compel the broker to
obtain execution at the exact stop price. It only releases the order for execution as a market order at the best possible price
obtainable.

You can also place a limit order stop loss. In this case,
you have instructed your broker to sell AU Corporation at no
less than $7.00 a share. With a limit order stop loss, you are
not guaranteed of getting out of your stock position. For instance, if AU Corporation dropped from 7 3/8 to 6 3/4, your
order to sell at 7 would never be executed. For this reason,
market stop loss orders are preferable. Remember, you are attempting to protect your gains as best you can.

With your market order stop loss at $7.00 a share, you
have protected a profit of $1,000 or $1.00 a share. Should AU
Corporation continue to rally, you can cancel the $7.00 stop
loss and set another one at a higher price. If AU Corporation

does drop to $7.00 a share, your stop loss will kick in, insuring the sale of your stock at the next opportunity at the best available price.

Another way to use stop loss orders is with the purchase of new stocks in your portfolio. You invest in a stock with the anticipation of price gains, but you don't want to hold onto the stock if the gains don't materialize. You can place a stop loss order at several dollars per share below your purchase price to insure getting out of the stock before it takes a drastic tumble.

Of course, only you can determine the amount of risk you want to assume. Each particular stock investment is unique and your stops must be set accordingly. Certain stocks are known for trading in ranges and you would not want to set your stop loss within that trading range pattern.

Discipline enters the picture by determining what profit or loss percentage you are willing to live with and setting appropriate stop loss orders to protect your gains and safeguard against catastrophic losses resulting from hesitation or indecision. Many investors fool themselves into believing they have the self-discipline to enter their own sell orders without the need for stop loss orders. A quick review of your past trades and how their results compare with your expectations may shed some light on your degree of discipline. Be objective, give the stop loss tool a fair hearing. It could mean the difference between capital gains and losses on your tax returns.

Stocks listed on the New York and American stock exchanges have their stop loss orders executed according to exchange rules. With over-the-counter stocks, however, you must count on the efficiency of your broker to monitor the OTC stock's price and enter a sales order when the specified price is met. Don't be bashful about calling your broker to make sure the stop loss has been entered. Remember, it's your money.

TECHNICAL ANALYSIS An investment technique which analyzes market and stock prices and volume trends with the purpose of establishing buy and sell strategies. Technical analysts use charting and/or computer analysis programs to isolate price and volume movements which are believed to signal market and individual stock price movements.

Technical trading offers several advantages. Since timing is considered a key in making buy and sell decisions, a technical chart can signal an impending event, allowing the technician to buy before a substantial price rise or sell before a drastic price decline. Fundamental analysis is often too late with the news to be of any help in making investment decisions. For example, by the time a news release of increased earnings hits the street, the market has already discounted the news in the current stock price.

Charts are at the heart of technical analysis. Simply put, charts graphically display numerical information and in the process point out trends, relationships, and patterns. Technicians hope to be able to forecast market and stock price movements by studying the trends, formations, reversal patterns, resistance and support levels, gaps, and trend lines.

Chart watching is based on the premise that history will repeat itself in patterned movements. Analysis of past market and stock actions will help to predict the future. The theory is that if the stock or market is weak, the chart will reflect it. Conversely, if the stock or market is strong, the chart will reflect the strength as well.

Chart formations are endless. Some of the more common patterns are head and shoulders tops, double tops and double bottoms, ascending tops and descending bottoms, resistance levels and support levels, and saucers.

Besides charting price movements, technical analysts also study other technical conditions. For instance, volume is an indicator of the direction of the trend. Typically, volume is expected to rise in bull market rallies and decline on corrections. In a bear market, volume is expected to increase on downturns and decrease on upward corrections. Heavy volume at the end of a considerable price movement is taken as a signal that the end of the trend is near and a turning point is forthcoming.

Another tool watched by technicians is the breadth of the market. The number of advances and declines in a particular day and for a period of time can help detect market direction and turns in the direction of the market. The advance/decline figures reflect the supply/demand relationship for stocks. An increase in the breadth or number of issues traded is termed bullish in a rising market and bearish in a falling market. A market would be considered technically strong if on a particular day 700 issues advanced, 400 issues declined, and 200 issues remained unchanged.

The number of new highs and new lows is a further indicator of the magnitude of strength in market moves. For instance, a market in a upward price movement and an average of 60 new highs a day would be technically stronger than a market in a similar price movement but recording only 20 new highs a day.

ASE/NYSE volume ratios indicate the number of amateur speculators entering the market. When stocks are rising rapidly, more amateur speculators enter the market, usually seeking out the most volatile secondary stocks of riskier companies. Proportionately, the American Exchange has more of these lower priced stocks than the New York Stock Exchange. The approach of speculative excesses can be predicted by monitoring the ASE/NYSE volume ratio.

Short interest is generally seen as a sign of technical weakness since the short sellers are betting on a downturn. More importantly, the direction of the amount of short interest can be an important indicator of market strength or weakness. While a large amount of short interest may indicate bearishness, a rise in the market could cause a short squeeze and short covering could help drive up the market substantially.

While many strict fundamentalist investors have discounted technical analysis, it may be prudent to use technical analysis as an added tool to gain knowledge of the investment climate and factors affecting your investment decision.

TOPS AND BOTTOM There are various chart patterns that illustrate market tops and bottoms. Some of the more common patterns are described and illustrated below.

Chart 20 illustrates a support level for the stock around $22 a share. The market price hit $22 a share several times and then rebounded. Timing purchases to coincide with reaching support levels can help you catch the stock at its bottom, profiting on sales of the stock as the price rises above this support level.

Chart 20

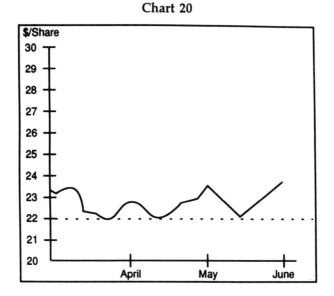

Chart 21 illustrates a resistance level for the stock around $27 a share. The market price has hit $27 a share several times followed by price declines. Timing stock sales to take place before the stock reaches a resistance level can help avoid the subsequent price decline and lost profits.

Chart 21

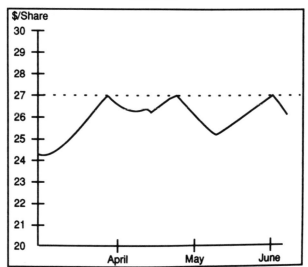

Chart 22 illustrates a typical double bottom pattern. The stock has hit the resistance level and rebounded. Getting aboard a stock that has exhibited a major bottom can be very profitable. A double bottom is usually taken to forecast a major change in direction and the end of a downslide.

Chart 22

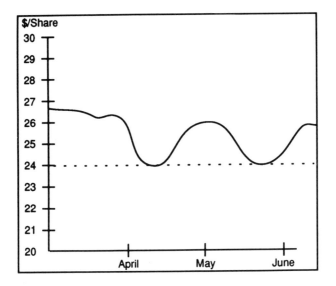

Chart 23 illustrates a typical double top pattern. The stock has reached the resistance level twice and declined. The double top is usually interpreted to forecast a major change in direction and the end of a major advance.

Chart 23

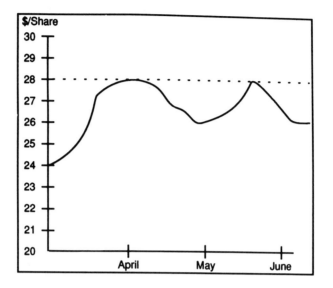

Charts 24 and 25 illustrate breakouts through resistance and support levels. A breakout confirmed by increasing volume signals a sharp price movement in the direction of the breakout. Often the breakout will be followed by a brief pullback to the resistance or support level before proceeding on to new advances or declines. The key is to move fast on breakouts. Early participation in a breakout through a resistance level can mean substantial profits, while waiting too long to act on the breakout through a support level can result in significant losses.

Chart 24

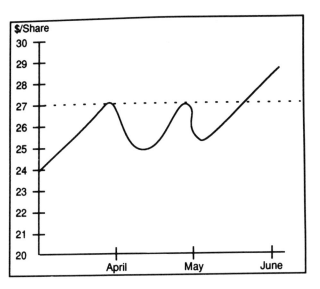

Chart 25

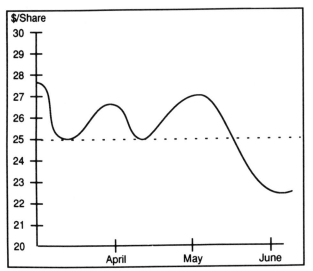

Chart 26 illustrates an ascending tops pattern. This pattern is considered bullish because each top is followed by another series of peaks, each higher than the previous one. Detecting an ascending tops pattern early will help to boost stock market return on your investment.

Chart 26

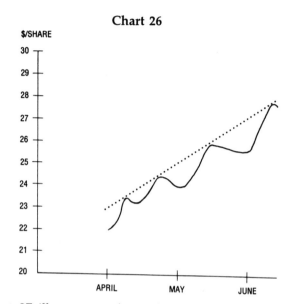

Chart 27 illustrates a descending tops pattern. This pattern is considered bearish because each peak is followed by a lower peak. Don't be fooled by a stock's apparent rebound if previous highs are not reached.

Chart 27

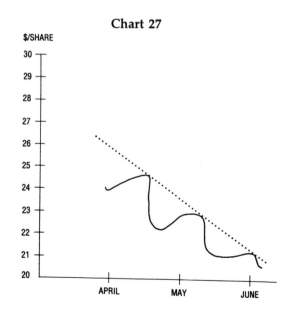

Charts 28 and 29 illustrate breakouts through descending and ascending tops. The breakout penetrates the trendline showing the direction of the stock pattern.

Chart 28

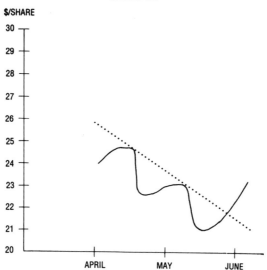

Chart 29

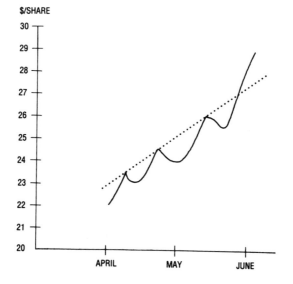

TRADING PATTERN The charted pattern of a stock or commodity which illustrates long-term direction and price movements. The slope of the parallel lines connecting the highest prices and lowest prices determines the overall price trend. For example, the trading pattern in the chart below illustrates a stock which trades in a consistent point spread range over several year periods with interim corrections to other levels.

Chart 30

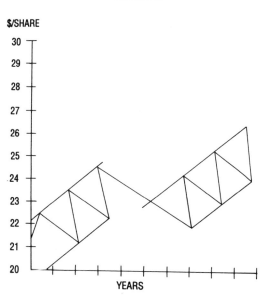

TRENDLINE Simply speaking, a trendline is a line drawn to delineate a trend. It is a straight line connecting the top or bottom market prices over a period of time. The trendline establishes the long-term price trend. Typically, trendlines connecting tops reflect declining prices while trendlines connecting bottoms reflect rising prices. The steepness of the trendline is important. A stock that has run up substantially within a short period (a steep trendline) is bound to run out of steam and may topple just as fast.

It is also important to pay attention to the number of times the trendline has been tested. For example, a trendline with four or five bottoms along its rise has greater holding power as a trend predictor than one which has only two bottoms supporting the rise.

TURNAROUND A turnaround is a positive change in the fortunes of a company which can result from many factors. A major mineral find, new management, technological breakthroughs, and new product lines can set the stage for dramatic turnarounds.

Investors adept at locating turnaround situations can far outperform the market. Turnaround investing takes research, time, patience, and an element of risk. When an apparently terminal company turns around, the profits can be astounding. A classic example—Chrysler stock languished below $2.00 a share before Lee Iacocca took on the Herculean task of reshaping Chrysler into a viable contender in the world automobile market.

Turnarounds offer special situations where you will be able to profit due to new and unusual developments within a company or in its surrounding environment. The profits come when the general market fails to recognize the significance of the event, thereby creating an undervalued opportunity.

Unlike many other special situations where the small investor finds out about them after the news breaks and the stock has already run up, turnarounds occur over a period of several months and frequently years. This allows you plenty of time to take your position in the stock at low prices. Turnarounds fit independent investors willing to analyze a company and make a decision based on that analysis.

Several elements make the turnaround attractive for small investors. First, the firm's stock usually remains severely undervalued as a result of substantial losses in recent periods. Second, many such firms sell below book value, meaning you will have some protection in the event the turnaround is not successful. Third, while losses accumulate, there will be low institutional participation in the stock. This provides the opportunity for quick upward movement as the institutions become aware of the successful turnaround and higher earnings spreads. Fourth, ample time exists for your analysis of the company—your study can be thorough before you invest.

The corporate turnaround, where a near bankrupt comany beats the odds to become a winner again, is one type of special situation where the individual investor can beat the institutions to the punch and earn substantial profits in the process. How often had you wished you purchased Chrysler stock in the pre-Iacocca days or bought a stake in beleaguered Republic Airlines before Stephen Wolf took the helm and effected one of the airline industry's most dramatic turnarounds?

Both Iacocca and Wolf saved the respective companies that hired them to get the job done but they also made a fortune for investors who were shrewd enough to recognize the signs of a successful turnaround in the making.   Chrysler stock could be purchased around $3 a share during the darkest days of the early 1980's. A $3,000 investment for 1,000 shares would have grown to 2,225 shares following 3-for-2 splits in March 1986 and April 1987. Just before the October 1987 crash, the $3,000 investment peaked at $106,800. Even as the stock drifted lower in the late eighties and 1990, the investor could have sold the shares at a substantial gain.

Republic Airlines common stock traded at $3 a share while its convertible bond only commanded $550 for every $1,000 bond on the New York Bond Exchange before Wolf was hired to pull the faltering airlines out of its fatal tailspin. Wolf instituted strict financial controls and slashed operating expenses. Labor contracts were negotiated and more fuel efficient aircraft brought on board to lower high fuel costs.

New route structures brought in needed revenues and helped capture market share. With the Wolf engineered sale of Republic to Northwest Airlines, the stock could be converted to $17 a share and the convertible bonds reached $1,270 per $1,000 bond before being called in by Republic.

More recently, the Irvine, California-based engineering and construction giant Fluor Corporation suffered losses in 1985 totaling over $630 million or $8.01 a share. Major turnaround restructuring efforts included shedding the firm's zinc operations, gold properties and drilling services segment. In addition, refocusing of business units sought out niche markets and refocused the company's core engineering and construction unit, Fluor Daniel.

The moves paid off handsomely by rebuilding revenues and bringing Fluor back into the black for the first time in four years with a profit in fiscal 1988. The firm is on track for further earnings gains with rising backlogs of work worldwide.

Astute investors who recognized the turnaround signs in place at Fluor participated in the rebound. From share price lows of $11 a share in 1986 and 1987, Flour's stock rose to a high of $49 1/4 a share in 1990.

Obviously, investing in corporate turnarounds can be very profitable, so why doesn't everybody do it? The answer is fairly obvious. There are two problems that face the turnaround shopper. The first is deciding which corporate turnaround to stalk. Not all turnaround attempts are successful and the losers can drain away your total investment in the company. Therefore, you must select your target carefully. The second problem is choosing the right investment strategy once the turnaround candidate has been spotted. Remember, it will do your finances no good if the turnaround is successful but the company's stock and/or bond prices don't advance.

Concentrate your search on industry smallfry or the giants of the industry. The smaller firms tend to be more flexible and can react quicker to changing conditions and market opportunities. The larger firms have the advantage of setting the pace while middle-sized firms are locked into pricing and policies set by the big boys.

Look for evidence of a major management shakeup. New managers are unburdened by ties to past decisions. Tiger International's hiring of Stephen Wolf paved the way for needed changes to keep the world's largest airfreight carrier from crashing. Keep abreast of management changes in the corporate elite as reported in *Barron's, Investor's Business Daily,* or *The Wall Street Journal.*

Wolf proved experienced in turnaround management. Wolf's brief tenure at Tiger International was long enough to effect a significant turnaround at its Flying Tiger operations before he was lured away by United Airlines parent Allegis Corp.

Once you've identified several likely prospects, take a look at the debt servicing and bank relationships that will be vital to the firm's survival. Request copies of the firm's annual report and 10k (the SEC required report with more detailed operating, financial and management information). A quick phone call to the company's public relations department or controller will get the reports in the mail. Be alert for new banking agreements, they reflect the degree of confidence the banks have in the firm's management.

Your broker is a good source of information on a company or industry. Read up on industry research reports and request copies of the S&P tear sheets of the companies that interest you. Most libraries carry a copy of *Value Line Investment Survey* and other stock research information.

While the financials will help you get a picture of the company's present situation, it will be outside economic forces and management's strategy that will help pave the way for a successful turnaround. Typically, information on management plans and actions can be found reported in the business journals. Division sales or shutdowns, personnel layoffs, and corporate restructurings are signs of a turnaround strategy in action.

It is a good idea to concentrate on firms that have had a series of losses which help to shelter earnings due to tax credits. Lower priced stocks enable you to purchase more shares and reduce your total monetary risk for a specific number of shares, meaning you have better leverage.

Remember, top management changes signal that the firm is serious about trying to change its fate.

Once you have decided on your turnaround candidate, it is time to decide on your method of investment. In some cases, there may only be common stock available and your choice is made for you. More often than not, companies in financial trouble have gone to the debt markets for financing and have had to offer "kickers" to entice investors. These kickers may be attractive convertible options or higher than market interest rates.

Convertibles have a distinct advantage over common stock since the common dividends are usually suspended by the company's board during troubled times. Convertibles offer the investor the possibility to earn above average yields while waiting for the new management to turn the firm around plus provide for participation in the rise of the common stock as the investing public and institutions take notice of the firm's changed fortunes.

They also offer some protection on the downside, if the common stock price drops, the convertible should decline less dramatically because the interest income offered by the bond will help support its price. One other advantage, if the company should enter bankruptcy, bonds hold a more secure position than common stock in the courts.

An excellent source for finding out about specific convertibles is *Value Line Options & Convertibles*. Regular listings and prices of convertibles appear in the major investment publications.

Pay close attention to the conversion and call features in the bond indenture. Some investors have been burned when they have paid a premium for a bond only to have it called in by the company at a lower price.

The individual investor has an advantage over large institutions because fund managers typically like to see clear evidence of the turnaround before investing funds in the company. An astute investor backed by a little investigative legwork can establish a position in a turnaround stock before the institutions drive up the price.

A final caveat—remember, not all turnarounds will be successful, but one solid turnaround investment can make a substantial difference in your portfolio results.

Your analysis will be the key to profits. To illustrate which elements you'll need to examine, a review of the General Refractories Company turnaround is in order. The turnaround began with a sweeping management change survival strategy implementation. In this particular case, the analysis stretched over two years during which time there were at least five major buying opportunities offering an 18% return on each investment.

Since turnaround situations are companies which have suffered financial setbacks, resulting in depressed stock prices, a good place to start your analysis includes a review of companies in depressed industries or cyclical industries nearing the bottom of their economic trough.

In 1982, the mining, construction, and steel industries experienced a sharp recession. It was a logical place to search for a turnaround. The financial press regularly publishes articles on industries and laggards within the industries. Start a file for potential turnaround candidates.

In the case of General Refractories, it made sense to concentrate on a supplier of the steel industry because the fortunes of smaller, peripheral companies can make a more rapid turnaround than the large companies they serve. The review of General Refractories was prompted after it appeared in *The Wall Street Journal's* list of new price lows. A little research revealed that the company supplied refractory brick to the steel industry, filler and filter products to a variety of markets, and building materials to the construction industry.

Subsequently, an article in *Newsweek* reported on radical changes taking place at the company. Four new directors were placed on the company's board, lenders agreed to restructure credit arrangements, and salaried staff reductions were instituted at corporate headquarters.

General Refractories served a weak industry and was itself beleaguered. The opportunity for a turnaround was signaled by management actions. Best of all, the stock market failed to notice the opportunity as the low market price revealed.

In other words, the signals that will help reveal likely turnaround candidates are easily found—you need to go no farther than your library. It is also a good idea to concentrate on firms with recently declining earnings or a series of losses which will help shelter earnings due to tax credits. If you stick with the lower-priced issues, you will be able to purchase more shares and reduce your total monetary risk, meaning you'll have better leverage.

To refine your analysis, accumulate all the information on the companies and industries you are evaluating. Remember, you have time on your side. Annual reports will help you narrow the field. Pay close attention to the "Notes" section in which management will describe its plans to rescue the company. The SEC required 10k forms are very useful. They supply more in-depth financial, statistical, and management analysis information. This includes segment data about major products and significant activities in product lines, properties, legal proceedings, acquisitions, and divestitures.

Further information can be gained from corporate news releases and stock analysis services such as *Value Line* and *Standard & Poor's*.

For turnarounds, management change is the most visible indicator. New board members and new senior management will bring new ideas and strategies to corporate policy making. Ties to past decisions are severed, and efforts will be concentrated on making the company profitable again.

The July, 1982 *Newsweek* article provided the tip on Robert W. Smith, a retired executive vice president of U.S. Steel, taking the reins at General Refractories. He brought to the company sorely need financial expertise and knowledge of the steel markets the firm served.

General Refractories went on to recover and once again become a viable force in its industries. Management did what was needed to increase working capital while cutting operating costs. Look at management actions regarding plant closings and consolidations. Pay close attention to working capital and long-term debt. The financial community's confidence (or lack thereof) in a company will be reflected in the credit agreements and terms that are extended to the firm.

In addition, make sure that well-planned marketing initiatives in the company's area of expertise are underway. Such steps are obviously geared toward returning a company to profitability.

The point is this: financial ratios, balance sheet information, and income statement analysis will help you determine a company's financial picture at any given moment. But when you are looking for a turnaround situation, the key will be the management's actions and long-term strategies, most of which will be announced by the company.

Most importantly, have patience. It will take time to gather all the information you'll need, as does corporate restructuring. The market generally overlooks potential turnarounds until after the reversal is well underway, and the time and effort you give to your analysis can pay off very well.   When the stock price begins to reflect the return to profitability and future earnings growth of a much leaner, healthier company, you will discover the rewards can be substantial.

VALUE INVESTING An investment strategy aimed at finding quality investments in relation to the general market. Benjamin Graham, the father of value investing, differentiated between intrinsic value and relative value. Intrinsic value analysis attempts to value a stock independently of its current market price by reviewing the firm's assets, earnings, dividends, future prospects, and management talent.

Relative value analysis, on the other hand, compares the attractiveness of an individual stock in relation to earnings and dividend multipliers for a specific industry or other grouping.

Despite popular acclaim of the efficient market theory, many stocks will sell for less than they are worth. Fortunes can be made ferreting out those investment gems the market has overlooked.

The key component of stock valuation include expected future earnings, expected future dividends, capitalization rate (multipliers) of dividends and earnings, and asset values.

One of the signs of a quality company is an uninterrupted stream of dividend payments. Firms with at least 10 years of continuous dividend payments exhibit growth and stability. Capital structure and financial strength also warrant a look. A company with sufficient working capital can handle capital improvements, facility additions, and strategic acquisitions without resorting to high cost debt. The capital structure must be balanced to make effective use of leverage and maximize return on equity without undue risk.

Management makes up the final ingredient. Has management kept up with both manufacturing technology and the emergence of a global economy? Management of both the domestic auto and steel industries fell asleep at the switch, letting Japanese firms with more efficient, new technology eat away at domestic and world markets. New management can also turn a dog into a thoroughbred. Lee Iacocca at Chrysler proved this point.

There are specialized sectors of value investing that merit mention. Asset investing searches out companies with substantial assets worth far more than the company's market price. Examples include oil and gas reserves of natural resource companies, land holdings of railroads and utilities, and undeveloped land of real estate firms.

Company turnarounds, such as Chrylser, provide ample opportunity for stock gains. In these cases, greater weight is placed on management, underutilized assets, and market potentials than the company's earnings and dividend track records.

Anticipating takeover situations can be a boon to investment profits. Although presently sitting on attractive cash hoards, many companies can be even more valuable when broken up into smaller units than they are as a whole.

Spend the time to search out value and enjoy the rewards.

VERTICAL LINE CHARTING Technical analysis chart technique utilizing a vertical line to indicate the high and low trading range for the period and a horizontal line to indicate the closing price. Over time, the chart shows the stock trend.

Chart 31

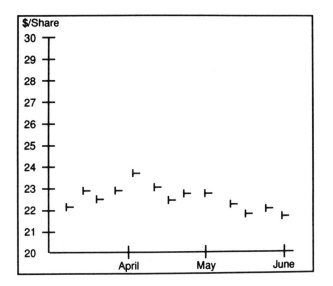

WARRANT A warrant is an option to purchase a stated number of shares at specified price within a specific period of time. In that respect, warrants are similar to options. But there are some unique differences.

First, a warrant is issued by the company whose stock is involved. Second, a warrant is usually issued to stockholders of record as of a certain date. Third, while an option has a life of a few months, a warrant may not expire for several years (usually five or ten years after issuance).

Corporations issue warrants for a variety of reasons. They can be used in place of cash or stock dividends to stockholders or as an incentive to participate in an upcoming issue. Often they are a "sweetener" to new debt or equity offerings—for example, to help obtain lower interest rates in the case of bonds or better acceptance of new equity securities. Warrants may be issued in connection with acquisitions and reorganizations or as partial payment to underwriters for services performed.

Warrants are traded on the NYSE, AMEX, and over-the-counter. As a warrant holder you have no equity rights in the company, do not receive dividends, and do not have voting rights.

A number of factors combine to affect a warrant's price. The maximum value of a warrant is the value of the underlying common stock; it will not exceed this value because the warrant offers no income potential beyond that of the common stock. The terms specified on the warrant certificate also affect a warrant's price. These include the number of shares that can be purchased with the warrant, the expiration date, and the exercise price. The exercise price is always greater than the current market price at issuance and can be fixed over the life of the warrant or adjusted periodically.

The warrant price is far from static. It is affected by the trading volatility of the underlying stock, the stock dividend, and prevailing interest rates. The value of a warrant increases with the increased volatility of the underlying stock since there is a greater chance of the stock increasing above the exercise price. The highly leveraged position of warrant trading is more valuable as interest rates rise; therefore, warrants command a higher premium during periods of higher interest rates.

There a number of advantages to purchasing warrants; your investment outlay is smaller than if you purchase the stock outright; your risk is limited to the warrant premium, usually far less than the cost of the underlying stock; through leverage, your profit returns will be far greater; a 10 percent rise in the stock price could generate a 40 percent rise in the related warrant; a bond purchased with warrants offer hybrid characteristics of the convertible with a kicker; it earns interest like conventional bonds, is exchangeable into stock like true convertibles—plus the warrants can be sold to raise cash.

Barron's and *The Wall Street Journal* provide lists of currently traded warrants. Look for the symbol "wt" (it designates which securities are warrants). Also, be on the lookout for "ww" (with warrants) and "xw" (without warrants); they designate how warrant-related securities are being traded.

WEDGE A wedge is a stock or commodity chart pattern resembling a wedge pattern. The wedge has its base facing left. Rising wedges are considered interruptions of a falling price pattern while falling wedges as interruptions of an upward price movement. The following chart illustrates a falling wedge interrupting a rising trend.

Chart 32

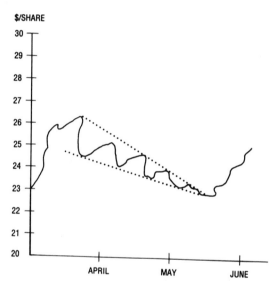

About the Author

Richard J. Maturi is a widely respected business and investment author whose nearly 1,000 articles have appeared in such distinguished publications as *Barron's, Investor's Business Daily, Institutional Investor, Your Money, Industry Week, Kiplinger's Personal Finance, The New York Times, Your Company,* and many others. In addition, he publishes three investment newsletters, *Utility and Energy Portfolio, 21st Century Investments,* and *Gaming and Investments Quarterly* (see discount coupon offer in back of book). Mr. Maturi is the author of *Stock Picking: The 11 Best Tactics for Beating the Market* (New York: McGraw-Hill, 1993); *Divining the Dow: 100 of the World's Most Widely Followed Stock Market Prediction Systems* (Chicago: Probus, 1993); *Money Making Investments Your Broker Doesn't Tell You About* (Chicago: Probus, 1994); and *The 105 Best Investments for the 21st Century* (New York: McGraw-Hill, 1995) *Main Street Beats Wall Street: How the Top Investment Clubs Are Outperforming the Investment Pros* (Chicago: Probus, 1995). Four of Maturi's books are Money Book Club selections.

Maturi is a member of the American Society of Journalists and Authors, Denver Press Club, and Wyoming Media Professionals. In addition to attending the University of Notre Dame, he received his bachelor's degree from the University of Minnesota-Duluth and his M.B.A. from Oregon State University. While in the corporate world, he managed company pension and profit sharing funds and served as a trustee of the Minnesota Teamsters Pension Fund. In 1993, Maturi travelled the Lincoln Highway route from Wyoming to Wall Street in his 1936 Oldsmobile, giving financial seminars and attending book signings en route. He and his wife, Mary, live in a log home in the Laramie Range of Wyoming's Rockies.

The author of *Wall Street Words* invites you to examine these three special offers:

Gaming & Investments Quarterly

Covers the gambling, hotel, and entertainment industries with in-depth analysis of unique common stock investment opportunities. Regular $75 annual subscription; special price, $25 annual subscription.

Utility & Energy Portfolio

Includes investment ideas, discussions of where to find higher yields and safety, plus coverage of major industry trends and key players. Regular $95 annual subscription; special price, $35 annual subscription.

21st Century Investments

New investment newsletter covering investment opportunities positioned to perform well into the next century and beyond. Regular subscription $95, special six month trial offer for only $5.

— — — — — — — — — TEAR HERE — — — — — — — — — —

Please send check or money order,
or order with your Discover® card:

R. Maturi, Inc.
1320 Curt Gowdy Drive
Cheyenne, WY 82009

☐   Gaming & Investments Quarterly @ $25

☐   Utility & Energy Portfolio @ $35

☐   21st Century Investments @ $5 (six month trial offer)

Name_____

Address _____

City _____ State _____ Zip _____

Account No. _____ Exp. Date _____